Gerald Griffin

(1803-1840)

A critical biography

Gerald Griffin

(1803-1840)

A critical biography

JOHN CRONIN
Senior Lecturer in English
The Queen's University of Belfast

CAMBRIDGE UNIVERSITY PRESS

Cambridge

London · New York · Melbourne

Published by the Syndics of the Cambridge University Press
The Pitt Building, Trumpington Street, Cambridge CB2 1RP
Bentley House, 200 Euston Road, London NW1 2DB
32 East 57th Street, New York, NY 10022, USA
296 Beaconsfield Parade, Middle Park, Melbourne 3206, Australia

First published 1978

Printed in Great Britain by
Western Printing Services Ltd, Bristol

Library of Congress Cataloguing in Publication Data
Cronin, John, 1928–
Gerald Griffin, 1803–1840.
Bibliography: p.
Includes index.
1. Griffin, Gerald, 1803–1840.

2. Authors, Irish – 19th century – Bibliography.

PR4728. C8Z58 · 823′.7 [B] 77–80831
ISBN 0 521 21800 4

To my wife, Joan, and my parents,
Jeremiah and Mary Cronin

Contents

Plates

Acknowledgements

I owe a special debt to Rev. Br. W. P. Allen of the Christian Brothers, North Richmond Street, Dublin, who is a lover of Gerald Griffin's works and cherishes his memory. He was most generous in supplying me with source materials and with his own copies of first editions of some of the novels. It is to him I owe my discovery of the interesting *Common-Place Book A*. Br. Allen also put me in touch with Rev. Br. L. A. O'hAnluain, then Superior of the Christian Brothers' Generalate in Rome, who most kindly searched the archives of the Order for the unpublished letters of Gerald Griffin. I am indebted to various people for help in finding suitable illustrations. These include Rev. Br. P. N. Dineen of the North Monastery, Cork; Mrs Olive Goodbody and Mrs Mary Shackleton of the Historical Library of the Religious Society of Friends in Ireland and Mr Philip B. Wilson of the Ulster Folk and Transport Museum. Mr Alf MacLochlainn, then Keeper of Printed Books in the National Library of Ireland, assisted by supplying a microfilm of *Adventures of an Irish Giant* from the copy of the book in the Joly Collection of the Library. I was also given helpful information when exploring the background to this novel by Mrs Gail F. Borden, Reference Department, Library of the Boston Athenaeum and Mr John Alden, Keeper of Rare Books, Boston Public Library.

Among my colleagues at the Queen's University of Belfast, Professor John Braidwood encouraged me throughout and helped with suggestions on many points of detail, while Dr David Farley-Hills was endlessly patient in proffering expert advice on the presentation of the material and also helped greatly by lending me his personal copies of the *Literary Gazette*.

The staff of the Library at the Queen's University of Belfast were unfailingly helpful and my particular thanks are due to Mr W. G. Wheeler, Mr M. L. Henry and Mrs Wendy McLaughlin. I also wish to record my grateful appreciation of the skilful and devoted work done by my subeditor at the Cambridge University Press in preparing a difficult typescript for the printers.

Grateful acknowledgement is made to the editors of *Eire-Ireland* and *Irish Booklore* for permission to reprint portions of the material which first appeared in the form of articles in those journals.

Abbreviations

Blackwood's	*Blackwood's Edinburgh Magazine*
Lit. Chron.	*Literary Chronicle and Weekly Review*
Lit. Gaz.	*Literary Gazette*
NLF	*News of Literature and Fashion*

Introduction

Gerald Griffin's reputation has remained high since his death in 1840, though few people would claim to know more of his works than his most celebrated and successful novel, *The Collegians*, first published in 1829. A notion of his special quality has persisted which is almost as much a tribute to his character as to his literary achievement. He occupies a special place in the national affections and is one of the few of the Irish nineteenth-century novelists never accused of misrepresenting his people or of distorting his material for an alien audience. Misgivings which might be voiced about Charles Lever or even William Carleton are never uttered about Griffin. Yet it would not be entirely adequate to dismiss all this as a kind of chauvinistic piety. There persists also the idea of a fine talent somehow shrouded in personal sadness.

The sizeable reputation which he earned with his fiction during his lifetime was given a fillip by Macready's successful production of his play, *Gisippus*, two years after its author's death. He continued to be commented on favourably and with a special warmth all through the middle and later part of the nineteenth century in the journals, in the memoirs of other writers and in histories of fiction and the drama. Inevitably the comment has tended to be repetitious since critics have had very little to go on apart from the works themselves. Griffin destroyed the bulk of his papers before he entered the Christian Brothers' teaching Order in 1838 and commentators have had to rely almost entirely on Daniel Griffin's *Life* of his brother for information about the man, his temperament and circumstances. This has tended to bolster Griffin's reputation as a sensitive and suffering soul, since Daniel's book is understandably gentle to its subject. Many of the notices in journals content themselves with a reiteration of the bare biographical facts offered by Daniel, along with a generalised tribute to the writer's charm and his sensitive delineation of Irish character. Although Daniel's comments on his brother are not as imperceptive as has sometimes been suggested, the real value of the *Life* lies in the considerable number of Gerald's letters which it preserves. Regrettably, however, these are not always dated and Daniel obscures the picture somewhat by his cautious use of initials in place of full names in many cases.

There has been surprisingly little in the way of critical commentary on the works of Gerald Griffin. Apart from the notice given to him periodically in the journals, his memory has been piously preserved by the Christian Brothers in a number of centenary papers and booklets which do little more than repeat a selection of facts from the *Life*. In 1940, the centenary of his death, this kind of activity produced a booklet by W. S. Gill which is little more than an extended pamphlet along the lines indicated. In 1954 Miss Ethel Mannin published the most considerable study of Griffin which had yet appeared when she made him the first of her two subjects in *Two Studies in Integrity*. This well-written and perceptive work concerns itself with the writer rather than with his writings and finely achieves its object of exploring Griffin's personality. Like her predecessors in the field, Miss Mannin is understandably dependent on Daniel's biography but she also had access to some shorthand notebooks and some unpublished letters in the possession of the Christian Brothers. Miss Mannin has made the most considerable contribution so far to the biography of Griffin. She has not, however, attempted any critical assessment of his fiction. Apart from hers the only work deserving of notice is the study of some of Griffin's novels contained in Thomas Flanagan's *The Irish Novelists 1800–1850*. This admirable pioneering work is a survey of the Irish historical experience in the first half of the nineteenth century. Flanagan examines a selection of the works of five of the novelists: Lady Morgan; Maria Edgeworth; John Banim; William Carleton; Gerald Griffin. In his three chapters on Griffin he examines *Tales of the Munster Festivals*, *The Collegians*, *The Rivals* and *Tracy's Ambition*, and finds Griffin a more 'native'

writer than Maria Edgeworth or Lady Morgan. He sees him as
the chronicler of a rural civilisation which was to fall to pieces
in the Great Famine a few years after Griffin's death. One
notices again in Flanagan's analysis the insistence on the special
Irish quality of Gerald Griffin which distinguishes him from so
many other novelists.

My interest in Gerald Griffin and his works arises in the first
place from my early education and from the historical and
literary assumptions of some of my early teachers. Chief among
these is Daniel Corkery, most celebrated of the modern Irish
critics with a strongly nationalistic bent. In his own way
Corkery has placed his stamp on a whole generation of Irish
minds just as F. R. Leavis has unmistakably shaped the thought
of another generation in England. I was, briefly, an under-
graduate during Corkery's last year as Professor of English at
University College, Cork, and I attended his lectures. I did not
get to know him personally, but the strength of Corkery's convictions combined with his considerable ability to produce on
the one hand a couple of notable apostates in Frank O'Connor
and Sean O'Faolain and on the other a flock of devotees and a
whole climate of opinion. It was in this climate that I received
my first critical direction in regard to Irish literature.

Broadly speaking, the fundamental assumption was that all
Irish writing in the English language was in some special way
suspect. A true Irishman would express himself in his native
Irish language, and if, through an accident of history, this
proved to be impossible, he would work to perfect himself in
the native tongue before attempting to express himself. This
linguistic purism made it difficult to cope with the nineteenth-
century writers who had come into being just as the Irish
language was going into a rapid decline and ceasing to be the
language of a majority of the people. The simplest critical
approach to adopt in these circumstances was to divide into
two broad categories those novelists unfortunate enough to
have been forced to write about Ireland in an alien tongue.
These categories might for convenience be labelled 'Ascendancy'
and 'native' writers. Among the former would be found Maria
Edgeworth, Lever, Lover, and Somerville and Ross. Among the
latter would be numbered such figures as Griffin, Kickham and

Canon Sheehan. Corkery's own attitude is cogently enunciated
in the opening chapter of his *Synge and Anglo-Irish Literature*,
where he describes Griffin as 'the type of the non-Ascendancy
writer who under the stress of the literary moulds of his time
wrote Colonial literature'. Later in the same work he distinguishes Griffin from Maria Edgeworth by reference to a
distinction between the 'suffrages' by which their work survives:

> *Castle Rackrent* for instance lives by English suffrage, but Gerald
> Griffin's *The Collegians* lives by Irish suffrage. Again, the work of
> Somerville and Ross lives mostly by English suffrage, while Carleton's
> work – written quite obviously under Ascendancy influence – lives
> by Irish suffrage.

This notion of 'suffrage' seems to connote for Corkery a subtle
amalgam of the writer's attitude to his material and his conception of his audience. The essential point is that one does not have
to disagree with Corkery's definitions to find the categories unsatisfactory. The real trouble is that the categories he defines
take no account of literary quality so that it becomes difficult to
establish one's emotional attitude to a fine novelist like Maria
Edgeworth as against a weak one like Kickham. Critical honesty
pulls one way, historical allegiances another, and the result of
all this is that genuine criticism of the Irish nineteenth-century
writers has been very rare. Irish critics have all too often
seemed to feel that they were improperly occupied in considering
these writers at all, and even the better articles in the more
responsible journals are often spoilt by the application of critical
standards of an extra-literary kind. Too much time and energy
have been spent in the definition of what constitutes Irish
writing. Too much fuss and fury have been devoted to trivial
questions of terminology while critics worried about the meaning of 'Anglo-Irish' and side-tracked themselves into all sorts
of fascinating but essentially irrelevant by-roads. It is from this
kind of futility that one turns in relief to exploratory work such
as Flanagan's, and my own reaction was, understandably, a
consuming curiosity about novelists who had been so unfairly
neglected. In a sense, then, my first curiosity about Gerald
Griffin was of the Himalayan kind. That is to say that I tackled
him 'because he was there', there at the very beginning of his
troubled and troublesome century, close in time to the native

tradition I had been taught to revere, but linguistically separated by accident of birth and history from 'the hidden Ireland'
and forced to come to terms with his own time and his own
future.

My interest was given a new stimulus when I was devising a
course in Anglo-Irish fiction as an option for the B.A. Honours
degree at the Queen's University of Belfast. I came to see that
Griffin is important as the first native Irish novelist of genius
and that he has a seminal interest as one of the first of a long
series of talented *emigré* writers. I began to be interested in him
as a writer caught between a nostalgia for a dying Ireland
and an intellectual inclination towards the new Anglicised
Ireland. His career, with his early emigration to London, his
subsequent revulsion against that city and all it signified, and
his decline into a ruinous moral scrupulosity, seemed to me to
embody certain important kinds of Irish response to the modern
Irish experience, and not only to afford an important point of
entry into the Anglo-Irish literary tradition but also to have a
good deal to say to the modern Irishman trying to come to
terms with a confused inheritance. Logically, therefore, a good
deal of my curiosity centred on Griffin's early adult life in
London, a period previously unexplored, and I decided to try to
trace as many examples of his journalistic work as possible. I
was curious about this work because I wanted to discover what
a talented young Irishman could offer to the London public in
the 1820s, and I also wanted to find out the writer's attitude to
the Londoner on the latter's home ground as compared with his
attitude to an English audience in his novel writing. My concern
here was with the Anglo-Irish writer's problem of tone and with
the regional writer's need to exploit an exotic subject-matter
for an alien audience. I think I can claim to be the first collector
of Griffin's journalistic work and I hope to have filled a gap in
his story by uncovering at least some of the writings by which
he earned his living during his London period. As I try to show
in Chapter 2, this journalistic work provides a vivid example of
the early expatriate Irish writer functioning in an alien environment and adopting a variety of *personae* to accommodate the
disparities of his audience and his material.

I was also eager to attempt some sort of full critical survey

of the fiction, including the play, *Gisippus*. What most interestingly emerged when I came to attempt this was that the work,
apart from its essential literary and historical interest, throws a
most revealing light on the writer himself. The novels provide a
revealing insight into Griffin's psychology and help towards an
understanding of his creative development and decline. In this
connection, I have made use of a common-place book of Gerald
Griffin which had not previously been noticed or studied. I found
it at the Christian Brothers' house in North Richmond Street,
Dublin, where Griffin was received as a novice in 1838. Br.
W. P. Allen kindly lent me the manuscript and permitted me to
study it and make extracts from it. There is an extended commentary on *Common-Place Book A* and its relevance to the
historical novel, *The Invasion*, in Chapter 5. In addition, I also
uncovered several other interesting items previously undis-
covered or ignored. The largest of these is the forgotten novel,
Adventures of an Irish Giant, first published in serial form more
than a decade after the writer's death, in *Duffy's Fireside
Magazine*, and afterwards in book form in Boston. This has
been considered in an Appendix since it proved impossible to
date it with certainty and my aim elsewhere was to examine the
fiction chronologically. In the course of my researches I also
found two previously uncollected stories which had been first
published in the London annual, *The Literary Souvenir*. These
are noted in the Bibliography.

I was particularly anxious to trace the unpublished letters
which had been made available to Miss Mannin in 1954, and to
which she refers in the Preface to her *Two Studies in Integrity*.
These papers proved elusive as the archives of the Christian
Brothers had been transferred from Dublin to Rome some years
ago. I was given every possible assistance by the various houses
of the Order to which I directed my enquiries and particularly
by the Christian Brothers' Generalate in Rome. The letters
finally came to light in the archives in Rome and I was permitted
to publish them in the journal, *Eire-Ireland*, and to make use
of them in my study. I have also collected for the first time a
large number of critical and biographical articles on Gerald
Griffin and a full list of these is contained in the Bibliography.

As my work progressed I found that my respect for Gerald

Griffin's talents as a writer increased as did my awareness of his creative dilemma, historical, social and linguistic. I came to see him as a gifted creature in troubled search for his identity as an artist and as an Irishman. More and more I concluded that he takes his proper place as one of a long line of talented, insecure, expatriate Irish writers. I hope my study will be of some service in indicating this evaluation of Gerald Griffin and that it will be of interest also for the new material I have uncovered or collected.

Textual note

The Life and Works of Gerald Griffin (8 vols.) were published in
London in 1842–43. There is no evidence that Griffin himself
had played any part in the preparation of this series. The work
appears to have been supervised by his brother, Daniel, who
contributed Vol. I, *Life of Gerald Griffin Esq.* Such revision as
took place seems to have been undertaken by Daniel Griffin. In
the biography he mentions (on p. 324) a substantial alteration
which he made to the story, *The Barber of Bantry.* He also
altered the contents of Vol. V, *Holland-Tide,* omitting three of
the stories contained in the first edition of 1827 and adding four
stories not included in the first edition. The stories omitted were
St Martin's Day, The Persecutions of Jack Edy and *The Unburied
Legs.* Of those added to the volume, *The Barber of Bantry* and
The Village Ruin were taken from *Tales of My Neighbourhood*
(1835), *The Rock of the Candle* from *The Literary Souvenir* (1829),
and *The Knight of the Sheep* from *Heath's Book of Beauty* (1841).
Sadleir's account of these variations (in *XIX-Century Fiction,*
I, 157) is incomplete. He does, however, indicate that the *Life
and Works* are hard to come by and that several important works
were omitted from the series. These are *The Christian Physiologist* (1830), *The Invasion* (1832) and *Tales of My Neighbourhood*
(1835).

   Thus, the *Life and Works* (1842–43) have no special authority,
are in some respects misleading and are difficult to come by.
As the aim of the present work is to treat Griffin's work chronologically, in an attempt to indicate his development and
decline, it has been thought best to refer throughout to the first
editions of the works, unless otherwise indicated. These are
listed in the Bibliography. An important exception has been

made in the case of the *Life of Gerald Griffin* where the second edition has been preferred to the first. Daniel Griffin's Preface to the second edition indicates that it contains important revisions and corrections, as well as extra letters which were not in his possession at the time of the publication of the first edition in 1843. Reference to the *Life* is, therefore, to the second edition published in Dublin in 1857, unless otherwise indicated. Griffin's letters have been reproduced as they appear in the *Life* and, in a few cases, from the originals in the Christian Brothers' archives. When writing to his family and friends, Griffin does not strive for formal perfection of style or presentation. His occasional trivial errors of spelling and syntax and his informal punctuation (dashes in place of commas, for example) have not been regularised. Similarly, no corrections have been made in quotations from the published work. Since it has proved impossible to establish the exact date of *Adventures of an Irish Giant*, this novel has been dealt with in an Appendix.

1

The period, family background
and early life

The Ireland into which Gerald Griffin was born in 1803 was a
country which had recently, by the Act of Union, been firmly
relegated to colonial status. The effort of the 'Protestant Nation'
to define itself during the period of Grattan's Parliament from
1782 to 1800 had failed; the effort of the Catholic nation to
emancipate itself was under way. Griffin's life span lies between
the Union and the Great Famine, the period of the struggle for
Catholic Emancipation and the rise of O'Connell. The year of
his birth was also the year which saw the last despairing flash
of the republican defiance of 1798 quenched in the tragic death
on the scaffold of Robert Emmet, 'the darling of Erin'.

Griffin's life falls into the first four decades of post-Union
Ireland, a period of national anti-climax in which the Catholics
began painfully to awaken to the sad error they had made in
heeding the blandishments of Pitt, who had told them that their
wisest course lay in freeing themselves by a Union with England
from the bigoted domination of the Irish Protestant Ascendancy.[1] They were to discover their mistake as, for a generation,
Relief Bill after Relief Bill was blocked at Westminster. For
Ireland this was to be an era marked by intense agrarian dis-
content and by several hideous dress rehearsals (for example in
1817 and 1822) for the terrible potato famine which was to
strike five years after Griffin's death. It is the period which saw
the rise of terrorist bodies like the 'Whiteboys', 'Shanavests' and
'Caravats', and other such peasant organisations protesting
against tithes, rents and their other oppressions. Grattan, the
greatest figure to survive the closing of the Parliament in College
Green, carried on his unavailing struggle for Catholic rights at

1

Westminster, but gradually the control of the Catholic cause was to pass into the powerful grasp of Daniel O'Connell, whose efforts were to culminate in the granting of Catholic Emancipation in 1829, the year which saw the publication of Griffin's most celebrated novel, *The Collegians*. The book provides a richly illustrative cross-section of the Ireland of its day: at the top, the irresponsible and venal petty gentry represented by the Hepton Connollys and the Hyland Creaghs, drinking and duelling their heedless way to ruin; the decent, respectable, middle-class Daly family with a comfortable home and a son at Trinity College; the sturdy 'Milesian', Myles of the Ponies, living a kind of stern Arcadian existence on the Kerry mountains, and the peasantry represented on their more jovial side by Lowry Looby and more menacingly by Poll Naughten and her brother.

At the time of Gerald Griffin's birth, Ireland was painfully recovering from the effects of the penal legislation of the previous century. The full vigour of the Penal Code had been applied to Ireland during the eighteenth century. Writing to Sir Hercules Langrishe about this infamous body of law, Edmund Burke described it as follows:

You abhorred it, as I did for its vicious perfection. For I must do it justice: it was a complete system, full of coherence and consistency, well digested and well composed in all parts. It was a machine of wise and elaborate contrivance; and as well fitted for the oppression, impoverishment, and degradation of a people, and the debasement in them of human nature itself, as ever proceeded from the perverted ingenuity of man.[2]

Catholic landowners were systematically deprived of their lands and of any chance of ever regaining them. The Penal Code saw to it that Irish Catholic landlords who might constitute a threat to the Protestants who had displaced them were transported to the colonies.

The Act of 1703 in Ireland provided that the fee-simple lands of all Papists were to descend equally to all the sons by gavelkind and not by entail to the eldest son (that is, the law required that land be bequeathed to all sons in equal portions). This split up the Catholic holdings. If the eldest son of a Catholic conformed to the Protestant religion he obtained the fee-simple in reversion of the land while the father retained only a life-interest without the right to settle the land on younger children. If the wife of a Catholic landowner conformed, she could obtain from the Lord Chancellor a portion of the inheritance not exceeding one-third, and had full power to assign it. Even a younger son who conformed could force his Catholic father to disclose the value of his estate and could then obtain such portion for his maintenance as Chancery would decide. Catholics were forbidden by law to purchase land on long leases and were deprived of all rights in respect of land mortgages. Arthur Young and other observers were shocked by the appalling conditions prevailing in the country. If a Catholic improved his land to a point where profits were one-third more than the rental, any Protestant could obtain possession of the improved land. This naturally acted as a powerful disincentive to Catholics and soon landlords began to find that this vicious system was ultimately unprofitable to themselves. As a result, there was a general conversion from farming to grazing, tenants were forbidden to plough their lands and whole villages were evicted at the landlord's will. Gwynn sums up:

So it was a peasantry forced down to the last verge of destitution and degradation – dispossessed, proscribed, hunted off the fertile lands to give place to sheep and cattle, forbidden to improve their lands, exploited by the merciless agents of absentee landlords – who had to undertake the struggle for their own emancipation. They had been deliberately deprived of all education, and the great majority of Catholic peasants could not even speak or understand English.[3]

It is this desperate peasantry and their irresponsible overlords who figure in Griffin's novels. The peculiar, drear bleakness of many of his scenes and settings reflects calculated degradation of the Catholic majority by a vicious and selfish Protestant Ascendancy group. Burke had remarked the 'vicious perfection' of the penal system and the phrase is a good one. The aim of the system was nothing less than the degradation of an entire nation. Catholics were legislated against on matters affecting land, property, trade, education, the professions. Only in commerce did Catholics, here and there, begin gradually to amass some wealth and achieve some influence. Forced off the land, deterred from improving their holdings by fear of eviction and extortionate rents, the Catholics turned to grazing cattle and gradually began an export trade. Thus, as Gwynn indicates, a new Catholic middle class began to emerge:

It was from this trade that the wealthy class of Catholic merchants grew up, who were to be the leaders of their own people in the struggle for emancipation . . . in Cork, Limerick and Waterford . . . there came into existence a new class of prosperous Catholic merchants who, being prevented by law from investing their money in land, were obliged either to spend their profits on developing their own business, or else to emigrate and settle in other countries where Catholics enjoyed freedom. The rise of this new Catholic merchant class was to be the means of liberation for the Catholics who had been subjected to such a completely organised system of persecution.[4]

Gerald Griffin's father belonged to this new Catholic merchant class, though he cannot be said to have prospered mightily. It was this class of Catholic merchants who were responsible for the founding in 1756 of the first Catholic Association. The last quarter of the eighteenth century saw the gradual easing of the more vicious of the anti-Catholic laws, a process which began effectively with Gardiner's Relief Act of 1782. Irish Catholics were gradually emerging from the period of their darkest oppression, gradually being permitted to own land and to possess some sort of civic existence for the first time in over a century, though full political and parliamentary emancipation was still a long way off. In the sphere of education, too, things were gradually improving. The Act of 1782 permitted Catholics to teach, though only on certain pretty stringent conditions. The Catholic schoolteacher had to take an oath of loyalty to the Crown, could not have Protestant children in his school and was not allowed to teach in a Protestant school. Before a teacher could set up his school he was required to obtain a licence to teach from the Protestant bishop of the diocese or his representative. No 'popish university or college' could be endowed nor could any Catholic school be endowed. The Relief Act of 1793 removed the formal requirement in regard to licences, though they were still frequently issued in later years. This important Act also enfranchised the forty-shilling freeholders who were later to prove so vital in Daniel O'Connell's Clare election of 1828. In 1795 the Catholic ecclesiastical seminary at St Patrick's College, Maynooth was opened.

Thus Griffin was born into an Ireland where it was at least

possible for a Catholic to acquire some schooling legally, though
a mass of petty and irritating restrictions remained. He grew up
in an Ireland which was bidding farewell to its Gaelic past and
turning more and more to the English language and customs.
Great Irishman as he was, O'Connell, though himself a native
speaker of the Irish language, regarded that tongue as a barrier
to Ireland's progress. Although he often addressed large gather-
ings in the Irish language he believed that Ireland's progress
required an abandoning of ancient allegiances, political and
linguistic. Old poetic hopes of a Stuart return must give way to
the practicalities of Emancipation politics and the people must
learn the language of the administration. This sea-change in the
Irish national life was taking place during Gerald Griffin's lifetime, and it is obvious, both from his work and from his letters,
that he was profoundly affected by it. He got his schooling in
the English language and, in a sense, belongs by environment
and education to the newly Anglicised Ireland which was
emerging as a consequence principally of the legislative Union
with England and the direction given to the Catholic movement
by O'Connell.

When Griffin left Ireland for London at the age of nineteen
he faced the task of making his way in the capital city of the
alien culture which was replacing his native tradition. He had
to work as a columnist for English weekly papers and suit the
taste of the town. A letter which he wrote from London in
December 1825 gives an account of a Catholic meeting at which
the principal speakers were Daniel O'Connell and his friend and
collaborator, Richard Lalor Sheil. Griffin's tone here is an
interesting mixture of involvement and a newly-acquired, cosmopolitan sophistication:

You have a queer notion on the other side of the water, that your
concerns are greatly thought about here. It is a doubt to me if the
'dear little island' were swallowed by a whale, or put in a bag and
sent off to the moon, if the circumstance would occasion any further
observation than a 'dear me', at one end of the town, and a 'my eyes!'
at the other, unless, indeed, among the Irish mining speculators, or
some gentlemen equally interested. In all that does not concern their
interest or their feelings, these are the most apathetic people breath-
ing. Yet all wish well to the measures when spoken of. I did not like
the display in the Freemason's Hall. O'Connell was too familiar –

offensively so – and as for Sheil . . . *he* was certainly, at least on this occasion, no orator. People have long since found out that wordiness to be nothing more than dull humbug. Besides, his exordium (to speak in his own way) was most ineffably silly.[5]

This nicely combines the point of view of the Irish Catholic who has recently left his troubled country with the cynicism of the expatriate who has learnt the extent of the average Englishman's indifference to Ireland and its affairs. We are listening here to the voice of post-Union Ireland. It must have irritated brother William to have the affairs of his 'dear little island' so summarily dismissed by a recently departed younger brother, but the letter gives a genuine sense of the enormous task which O'Connell faced in breaking down the barriers of English apathy and prejudice.

When Gerald Griffin returned home after the publication of *Holland-Tide* in 1827 he found an Ireland in which O'Connell's Catholic Association had mobilised the ordinary people of Ireland as a meaningful force for the very first time. They had succeeded in toppling Lord George Beresford from his safe seat in Waterford in the previous year and O'Connell's famous victory over Vesey Fitzgerald in the Clare election took place in the following year, 1828. In a letter written to his friend, John Banim, from Pallaskenry on July 4, 1828 Griffin writes with tremendous enthusiasm about the Clare election. All his metropolitan condescension is gone and is replaced by a fervent admiration for the people of his native province and the achievements of their leaders. Sheil, whom he had condemned so roundly in the earlier letter, is now as warmly commended:

The people have certainly proved themselves to be a most resolute set of fellows . . . They fill the streets more like a set of Pythagorean philosophers than a mob of Munstermen. I heard your friend Mr Shiel [*sic*] address them with great effect the other day, and think him incomparably the foremost orator among the liberators . . . I should like much to know what people say of the struggle in your part of the world.[6]

Here is a change indeed, with Gerald now in the position earlier occupied by his brother, soliciting information about London's views on Irish events and Sheil exalted from 'ineffable silliness' to 'the foremost orator among the liberators'. The comment on the orderly behaviour of the Munstermen who supported O'Connell

in his election campaign is particularly interesting for the light
it throws on Griffin's conception of the Irish character. It is
clear that he was profoundly moved by the spirit of order and
discipline which O'Connell had called forth from the ordinary
people of Munster, and something of his response comes through
shortly after in his depiction of the natural dignity of Myles na
Gopaleen in *The Collegians:*

> His figure was at once strikingly majestic and prepossessing, and the
> natural ease and dignity with which he entered the room might
> almost have become a peer of the realm, coming to solicit the *interest*
> of the family for an electioneering candidate.[7]

Griffin, after a brief and unsatisfactory experience of expatriate cosmopolitanism which evidently included a bout of
religious scepticism was, after his return to Ireland in 1827, to
become more and more conscious of the dire straits of his fellow
countrymen, more and more aware of his strong personal need
for a clear definition of national identity, a point which will
become clearer in the treatment of his novel, *The Invasion*, in a
later chapter. Even leaving aside his strong personal inclination
to the religious life, it is not without significance that when he
withdrew from the world he chose to join a community whose
declared object was the education of the Catholic poor. At the
end of his life, when he had been transferred to the Christian
Brothers' house at the North Monastery in Cork, Griffin wrote
to a friend in England a letter which again exposes his peculiar
intellectual tensions:

> I have since been enlightening the craniums of wondering Paddies in
> this quarter, who learn from me, with profound amazement and profit,
> that o-x spells ox; that the top of the map is the north, and the
> bottom the south, with various other 'branches', as also that they
> ought to be good boys and do as they are bid, and say their prayers
> every morning and evening, etc., and yet it seems curious even to
> myself, that I feel a great deal happier in the practice of this daily
> routine than I did while I was moving about your great city, absorbed
> in the modest prospect of rivalling Shakespeare and throwing Scott
> into the shade.[8]

His reference to 'wondering Paddies' has, to Irish ears, a ring of
almost alien condescension. His protestations about his content-
ment in the religious life would seem to be borne out by such

letters of the period as survive, and yet one wonders. Notice the intriguing phrase 'it seems curious even to myself', which seems to suggest that doubts remain, that some sparks of literary ambition yet survive unquenched. He might, in time perhaps, have found that the complete submerging of his creative gifts was neither possible nor desirable and might eventually, had he lived, have had to face up to his personal dilemma anew.

Ethel Mannin notices a passage in one of Griffin's letters to Lydia Fisher which seems to her indicative of an essentially middle-class, conservative viewpoint.[9] The letter was written in 1833 from Taunton where Griffin was collecting material for *The Duke of Monmouth*. It is a long letter which gives a lively account of Griffin's visit with his brother Daniel to Thomas Moore at Sloperton Cottage. Towards the end of the letter the following passage occurs:

Oh, dear, Lydia, why didn't you make the Whitefeet [*sic*] behave themselves? They have almost made me ashamed of my country; and general as the outcry is through England at this dreadful law they are making, I am almost tempted to wonder that we have any friends at all, when I hear of one murder after another being committed by these unhappy wretches. But I must not touch on politics; and don't you be offended at my calling you to an account about the White-feet.[10]

Miss Mannin sees this horror at the atrocities of the Whiteboys as the product of what she calls Griffin's 'strictly O'Connellite – that is to say conservative – middle-class point of view'. She points out that Catholic Emancipation had done nothing to alleviate the sufferings of the peasants (it had indeed been accompanied by the disfranchisement of the 'forty-shilling freeholders' who had principally brought it about). It had meant places in Parliament for some well-to-do Catholics while the miseries of the peasantry continued unabated and Coercion Acts provoked a desperate people to the only retaliation open to them. All this is true. Griffin did come from a middle-class background and, by 1833, was reasonably prosperous himself. He did not live the grim life of an Irish peasant, but the artist in him transcended his social limitations and reached out to an under-standing of and profound sympathy for the tragic dilemma of the Irish poor. A novel such as *Tracy's Ambition* makes perfectly clear his real grasp of the viciousness of the system of mis-management and exploitation which obtained in Ireland. Griffin may have disliked the Whiteboy atrocities and may have recoiled from them in respectable horror, particularly when he heard about them while he was travelling in England, where, presumably, such events would be seen as yet another example of Irish barbarity, but he knew well what the causes of such events were. When he writes on such themes his prose often achieves unusual satiric force and clearly expresses his profound personal resentment of the cruel indignities inflicted on his fellow-countrymen.

FAMILY BACKGROUND AND EARLY LIFE

In the first edition of his *Life* of Gerald, Daniel stated that the Griffin family was probably of Welsh origin, but he corrected this in a lengthy and rather apologetic footnote at the opening of Chapter 1 of the second edition of the work.[11] He also added to the second edition a lengthy Appendix which consists chiefly of information about the origins of the Griffin family, furnished to him by Professor Eugene O'Curry, 'the eminent Professor of Irish in the Catholic University'. This note, beginning from *The Book of Lecan*, identifies the Griffins as a Munster family of ancient origin, and finds them 'taking an important part in the civil wars of Clare, between 1260 and 1320'. References to the O'Griffys in the *Annals of the Four Masters* are described and we are told that the O'Griffys had possession of the townland of Bally Griffy down to the reign of James I. The final dispossession of the O'Griffys which took place in 1662 is recorded in a manuscript preserved in the Library of Trinity College, Dublin, a lengthy extract from which is quoted in the Appendix.

The more recent history of the family is traced in considerable detail by the Rev. M. Moloney in a valuable article written at the time of the celebration of the centenary of Gerald Griffin's death.[12] Moloney includes in his article a family tree beginning with the novelist's grandfather, James Griffin of Corgrigg (1730–98). The novelist's father, Patrick, was James Griffin's third son. Patrick married Ellen Geary, sister of John Geary, M.D., the leading Limerick physician of his day. Patrick and

Ellen Griffin had a large family and the future novelist was to begin his life as a member of a devoted and closely-knit domestic group. Patrick Griffin would seem to have left his father's house at Corgrigg as a young man and gone to live at Woodfield, County Clare. While living there he engaged in brewing and when he moved to Limerick he became manager of a brewery, in Brunswick Street (now Sarsfield Street). He had a house built near the brewery for his growing family and while this house was under construction he lived at Bow Lane, where his three youngest sons, Daniel, Peter, and (on December 12, 1803) Gerald were born. The family moved to the new house in Brunswick Street soon after Gerald's birth and it was at Brunswick Street that the two youngest sisters, Anne and Lucy, were born.

According to Moloney, 'of the nine Griffin boys seven grew to manhood, and there appear to have been at least five girls', so that Gerald was one of the youngest in a very large family. Gerald spent his early years at the house in Brunswick Street, but, when the brewing venture failed, his father moved the family back to the parish of St Mary's where they had previously lived (though not to the house in Bow Lane) and set about building a new house for the family at Carrowbane, near Loughill, not far from his own native place of Corgrigg. The Griffins moved to their new house, 'Fairy Lawn', in 1810 and lived there until 1820, so that it was in this house that Gerald's childhood and adolescence were passed. Daniel describes the household as follows:

The family at this time consisted of his father and mother, two elder sisters unmarried, two younger sisters before spoken of, Gerald and myself. His eldest brother, while yet a mere boy, had obtained a commission in the army, and was gone to join his regiment. The next was sent to sea as a midshipman in the Venerable, a seventy-four gun ship, then cruising with the fleet in the channel; and two others had been put to business in Limerick.[13]

'Fairy Lawn' was beautifully situated on a hill above the Shannon estuary, about twenty-eight miles from Limerick and the entire family seems to have welcomed the change from city life with huge delight. Daniel's account of the move indicates this clearly and stresses the importance for young Gerald of growing up in such a beautiful spot. It was here that his young poetic imagination was to have its first impressions of natural beauty imprinted upon it, and much of the delight he took in lake and river and mountain and wood, and which he conveys so often in his fiction, must have begun its growth in his mind at this time. A teacher who had a school at Loughill was engaged to teach the children for a short time in the morning before he went on to Loughill to undertake his main duties, and he sometimes came back in the evenings to continue his tuition. According to Daniel, he taught them to write out pieces from the poems of Shakespeare, Goldsmith and Pope, and Gerald seems, at this time, to have begun to acquire a particular fondness for Goldsmith's prose and poetry. The older sisters helped with the teaching of the younger children and gave them lessons in French. In 1814, when Gerald was eleven years old, he was sent to school in Limerick where his teacher was a Mr T. M. O'Brien who introduced him to the Classics for which he acquired, according to Daniel, a considerable fondness. When a young man named Donovan opened a school at Loughill, which was closer to 'Fairy Lawn', Gerald was removed from Mr O'Brien's establishment and sent to the more rough-and-ready school of Mr O'Donovan. Daniel suggests that it was from the contrasts between the more correct O'Brien and the unorthodox Donovan that Gerald derived the hilarious comedy of the celebrated 'Latin construe' scene in his novel *The Rivals* (1829).[14]

As can be seen, the young Griffin's early education was often of a scrappy and haphazard nature and this reflects both his father's declining fortunes and the whole character of Catholic primary education at this time. P. J. Dowling has indicated the slowness with which the Penal Code was relaxed in the educational field and how grudgingly the licensing of Catholic schools was handled:

It is extremely doubtful if hedge schoolmasters, or indeed if any, except a few, lay teachers sought licences to teach. The safety of the schoolmaster was in his obscurity. There was no certainty that the best qualified applicant would obtain a licence; and there was no guarantee that having obtained it he would be allowed to hold it. So it was that the Hedge Schools, often described by contemporary writers as 'unlicensed schools', were illegal schools till the passing of the Catholic Emancipation Act in 1829.[15]

Later in the same work Dowling indicates that 'there was no clear-cut distinction between the town or city "academy" and the hedge school proper. They shared the same character of illegality.'

The scrappy nature of Griffin's formal education was to have an important effect on his entire development. A humiliating part of his nineteenth-century Catholic inheritance, it must surely have contributed significantly to the almost pathological sensitivity of his nature. Much later, in London, in the very year which saw the publication of his best and most celebrated novel, *The Collegians*, he is found enrolling as a law student at the newly opened London University where he attended the lectures of Professor Amos. Daniel explains this step by referring to his brother's fears about the uncertainty of the thankless profession of letters:

he had seen from time to time such distinct signs of the fickleness of public taste as tended seriously to shake that security he had begun to feel with regard to literature as a profession. 'I should like, if possible,' he says, in a letter about this time, 'to commence the study of some profession that might at one time or another render me independent of this scribbling. The uncertainty of the life it has been my misfortune to adopt is horrible.'[16]

Shortly after this attempt to acquire a formal education at the age of twenty-six, Griffin embarked on the lengthy preparation for his historical novel, *The Invasion*, a task which took him to libraries in Dublin and elsewhere in search of material. His earnest and painstaking attempts at historical scholarship reflect once again the unsatisfied educational yearnings of a young man of talent to whom his origins had been less than kind.

Quite apart from this, however, his father's failure in business and the family's declining fortunes militated against him. Daniel's biography is indulgent to all members of the family but the Micawberish quality of Patrick Griffin shows clearly even through the following filial account:

Many a time have I seen him in those embarrassments, the distressing nature of which he was by no means insensible of, endeavour to quiet the apprehensions of my mother, who always felt them more acutely, by representing to her the inutility of grieving for evils that were inevitable. When reasoning failed, he sometimes tried to laugh her out of her despondency; and it was amusing to observe the slight toss of the head with which he gave up the contest, and the smile that played around his countenance, when he found both equally unavailing.[17]

Amusing it may have been, but the sad result of it all was that the family was to be split in two by the usual Irish economic solution of emigration. Patrick Griffin's eldest son, who had spent several years serving with the British army in Canada, returned to live with the family at 'Fairy Lawn' in 1817. He began to urge upon them the desirability of emigrating to Canada. Neither Patrick Griffin nor his wife Ellen was attracted by the notion of emigrating to a part of the world where the severity of the winters would have proved trying to ageing people like themselves but, in 1820, they agreed to leave Ireland for Pennsylvania where they gave their new home the name 'Fairy Lawn' in memory of the happy decade they had spent in the first house of that name. Not all the family emigrated, however. Daniel and Gerald remained behind along with Ellen, Lucy and Anne, as well as the older brother, William, who had already qualified at Dublin as a doctor. William now became the head of that part of the family to remain in Ireland. He left 'Fairy Lawn' for a house in Adare and his brothers and sisters joined him there.

The departure of both his parents and a large part of his family to America was the most shocking blow yet inflicted by a hard destiny on the seventeen-year-old Gerald. His nature was a combination of intense warmth and extreme reserve and only his family circle provided a setting in which he could be entirely himself. Gay and lively within it, as his letters show, outside it he was touchy and reserved, even suspicious. He was well aware of this aspect of himself and commented on it in a poem written soon after his arrival in London, at a time when he was feeling peculiarly desolate and despairing. One stanza reads:

> I have a heart: I'd live
> And die for him whose worth I knew –
> But could not clasp his hand and give
> My full heart forth as talkers do –
> And they who loved me – the kind few –
> Believed me changed in heart and tone,
> And left me while it burned as true,
> To live alone! – to live alone![18]

Apart from his immediate family, only the Fishers, the Quaker family with whom he was to become intimate at a later stage, ever won his trust fully – he was always a domestic rather than a social animal. He was never to see his parents again but his letters to them demonstrate his continuing devotion and he gave concrete expression to his regard when he presented to his father the entire sum of £800 which he earned from *The Collegians* in 1829, nearly a decade after the family's departure for America.

It was now necessary for Gerald, at seventeen, to decide on his future career. Not surprisingly, he thought first of following in the footsteps of his brother William and becoming a doctor. To this end, he seems to have spent some time in William's surgery, and Daniel gives an amusing description of an encounter between a patient and the totally unqualified Gerald who was sent for, one day when William was absent on a case:

Dr Griffin being from home, he was sent for to see a man who had hurt his knee severely. One of those empirics, known in the country by the name of 'bone-setters', had arrived before him. These persons assume an air of learning in their intercourse with the poor, and pick up technical terms, which they use with as much ease and confidence as if they were familiar with the deepest mysteries of the science. Gerald examined the injured limb with the timidity and diffidence which were natural to him, and which were heightened at this moment by his being placed under the severely critical eye of the bone-setter, who looked on in silence, and when his examination was entirely over, asked with an air of great gravity before all the people – 'Pray, sir, do you think the *patella* is fractured?' 'I was puzzled,' said Gerald, 'to think what answer I should give him, *for I did not so much as know what the patella was.* I kept looking at the limb, all the while engaged in trying to keep my countenance. At length I said as gravely as I could, and with perfect truth, "I do not *know* that it is", with which he seemed satisfied, so I recommended some soothing applications, and got out of the house as quickly as I could, to avoid any more of his learned questions.'[19]

Gerald was to make excellent use of such incidents in later years. One recalls particularly the amusing accounts of Dr Vanderkyst and Dr O'Gorman in *Adventures of an Irish Giant*.[20]

As his interest in a literary career increased, he gradually abandoned the idea of qualifying as a doctor. Perhaps the greatest influence upon him at this time was his first encounter with a fellow-countryman who had begun to make a name for himself in the great world of letters. John Banim, who was about six years Griffin's senior, had had his tragedy of *Damon and Pythias* produced at Covent Garden in May 1821, with Macready in the leading role of Damon and Charles Kemble as Pythias. Banim had written for the *Limerick Evening Post* (under the pseudonym 'A Traveller') some critiques of performances by the Limerick Thespian Society, and Griffin had met Banim on his occasional visits to Limerick. The Griffin family had admired Banim's pieces in the *Post* and young Gerald must have been moved to emulate the Kilkenny man's London literary success. He had already had his first practical experience as a working journalist when he had briefly managed a Limerick paper called *The General Advertiser* for its proprietor, a Mr McDonnel. When an editorial written by the young Griffin evoked the displeasure of the authorities his contact with the paper ceased after a month. Before leaving, he made amends to the proprietor by writing a laudatory piece on the Lord Lieutenant, the Marquis Wellesley. 'It was my first step,' he said, 'into that commodious versatility of principle which is so very useful to newspaper writers, but it will be my last also.'[21] At this stage, he little knew what lay ahead of him in the way of journalistic hack-work for the London papers.

He now completed a full-length tragedy under the title *Aguire* (which has not survived) and showed it to William, who was impressed by the quality of the piece. Rather reluctantly, William agreed to let his younger brother attempt to make a literary career for himself in London, and Gerald set off for the capital in November of 1823. He was not yet twenty.

2

The London Period: 1823–1827

On arrival in London, Gerald submitted his tragedy, *Aguire*, to the judgement of a London actor at Drury Lane. Daniel makes the usual irritating deletion from the letter in which Gerald informs his brother William of this, so one cannot be certain who this actor was. There are, however, reliable indications that it was Macready. Macready had played Damon in Banim's *Damon and Pythias* shortly before and Griffin may have availed himself of his acquaintance with Banim to gain access to the celebrated actor-manager. A letter from Gerald to William indicates that the person to whom he submitted the play had been prevented from passing judgement on it by his involvement in James Sheridan Knowles's new play *Caius Gracchus*.[1] This play opened at Drury Lane on November 18, 1823, with Macready in the title role. Furthermore, in a letter to his sister, Ellen, on March 31 in the following year, Gerald, in recalling his disappointment, writes as follows:

—'s rejection of me I regard as a dispensation of Providence. I was a *leetle* too confident perhaps, and it was a seasonable humiliation in the commencement of my career. However, this does not excuse *him*. I do not say he might not have rejected me, but his manner of doing so was bad. He knew I was a stranger in London, young and inexperienced in such matters, and his countryman, and he kept me in suspense three months; then sent back my piece without comment, wrapped in an old paper and unsealed! If I had any wish for a little revenge – but I have not – I understand it will soon be gratified in some measure. The affair, without mentioning names, will be taken up in one of Blackwood's forthcoming Magazines.[2]

The 'Blackwood's' piece referred to here may be the ong letter signed 'Philo-Dramaticus', addressed to Charles Kemble and R. W. Elliston, which *Blackwood's* published in June of the

16

following year.³ This is a forthright attack on all the great
London actors of the day whose arrogant influence is said to
be the ruin of the London stage. Macready is singled out for
special condemnation in connection with his rejection of a
tragedy entitled *Rienzi* by an unnamed authoress who was, in
fact, Mary Russell Mitford. Although there is no definite indica-
tion that 'Philo-Dramaticus' is Griffin himself, the general
sentiments expressed in the piece in regard to the primacy of
the writer and the secondary importance of the actor are in his
vein. A commemorative article written just two months after
Griffin's death names Macready as the person to whom *Aguire*
was submitted. This article is unsigned, but an editorial note
ascribes it to 'the most authentic source', which may mean that
it was written by Daniel or William Griffin.⁴ Thomas Davis also
names Macready in this connection.⁵

At any rate, Griffin heard nothing further about his tragedy
for some time and, in the meantime, had to set about the business
of settling down in London. The November weather affected his
health adversely and he writes to William that he has had 'a
renewal of my old attacks of chest'. He was at first unable to
find Banim in London, though he called on Kemble and Young
to enquire his whereabouts. A friend with whom he had hoped
to stay let him down and so he had to write to William to ask
for money:

With respect to the situation of reporter, it is almost impossible to
procure it at present, as the business season has not commenced. That
of police reporter is easy enough, I believe, to be procured, but I am
told the office is scarcely reputable. I shall take a report of some
matter, and send it to the papers the first opportunity. I have had
such harassing work, looking after addresses, etc., together with
continued writing, and the terrible damp fogs that have prevailed
here lately, that I got this week a renewal of my old attacks of chest.
I am, however, much better. With respect to the state of my finances,
they are getting low.⁶

William, though himself suddenly afflicted by a serious illness
at this time, sent him money to tide him over his difficulties.

Gerald began to visit the London theatres where he found that
the most successful plays were those filled with grand scenic
effects of a most elaborate kind. He writes contemptuously to
William about the success of pieces such as *The Cataract of the*

Ganges, which filled Drury Lane for three weeks while *Venice Preserved* 'will scarcely draw a decent house'. Nevertheless, he set about writing into the second act of *Aguire* a grand procession and chorus, and set great hopes on 'the burning convent and the thunder storm' in his play. In December he writes of having seen Banim, who behaved with great kindness. He and his young wife made Griffin welcome at their home and Banim read through *Aguire* with him, approving of parts of it and making suggestions for alterations in other parts. 'I could not, on the whole, have expected Banim to act a more friendly or generous part than he has done,' Gerald writes to William on December 29, 1823. He was still dependent on William's financial assistance and the opening of the new year of 1824 brought a bad blow when *Aguire* was rejected and returned to him without comment. The letter of January 12, 1824, in which he writes to inform William of this disappointment, is full of wounded pride and a desperate desire to conceal his bitterness:

—has sent me back my piece (I don't like that word rejected), after keeping it nearly three months, without any opinion, other than the mere act of doing so. I had just the day before said to Banim, that I wished he would do it, for I heartily disliked the idea of his being considered my patron if he should accept it . . . of all actors I could have selected, — was the worst: for you must know he dabbles in tragedy himself, and I suppose you recollect the whisper to Sir Fretful, or Puff, (which is it?) in the Critic, – 'Never send a piece to Drury' – 'Writes himself?' 'I know it, sir.'[7]

The same letter also gives a clear hint of the unfortunate touchiness which was characteristic of Griffin in all his literary dealings and which was shortly to poison his relations even with the kindly and well-disposed Banim:

Banim said if I change the name, and make those alterations he pointed out, he will present it for me, and get me an immediate answer. I have not seen him since I wrote to you, for I was unwilling to be too troublesome to him, especially as he is himself constantly engaged. I let him know —'s decision, however, and have a letter from him by me, where, in answer to my question, whether I should send *Aguire* or another? he encourages me to do the former, but at the same time he leaves the *utrum horum* to myself. For many reasons I have chosen the latter. In the first place it would not be pleasant if — should recognise it at the theatre; secondly, it was known too generally that I was the writer; and lastly, Banim seems to think it better I should do so. With a true, indefatigable Grub-Street spirit, I have therefore commenced a new one, and have it nearly half-finished. The plot is that of Tancred and Sigismunda. Banim, I think would be apt to interest himself more in one which is written under his own eye. He says, at the conclusion of his letter, that if I give him a call he will speak about my commencing a connexion with the press in a limited way. I don't know what he means but I will see him this week.[7]

The play of Tancred and Sigismund he evidently abandoned on William's advising him that the subject was an old one and an unwise choice for a young author to undertake as his first presentation, but a letter of February 1824 indicates that he had already completed his play *Gisippus*, four acts of which he gave to Banim. He was at this time also associated with a Spanish friend, Valentine Llanos, in a project for translating Spanish works into English, and hoped to make some money on this. Valentine Maria Llanos y Guiterez, known as Valentine Llanos, had known John Keats in Rome and had visited him three days before his death. Llanos is mentioned frequently in Fanny Brawne's letters to Fanny Keats from the end of 1821 onwards. He married Fanny Keats in 1826.

The bleakest part of Griffin's London experience was now beginning and was to last for the first six months of 1824, until he began to make a little money by writing for various journals. During these six months he was impoverished and in poor health, depressed by bad news of his brother's illness and by the deaths of various relatives, oppressed by fears that he must inevitably fail to make any mark in the literary world and a growing conviction that he had embarked upon an impossible task in coming to London at all. In these dark days the most negative aspects of his character and temperament assumed the ascendancy in his relations with those who tried to come to his assistance. It is this period which aroused in him his loathing of London and the shifts and contrivances of the literary hack-work which was the lot of those who failed to make their mark rapidly. Writing to his parents at the end of the following year he can scarcely bear to describe his life at this time:

Until within a short time back I have not had since I left Ireland a single moment's peace of mind – constantly – constantly running backward and forward, and trying a thousand expedients, and only to meet disappointments everywhere I turned. It may perhaps appear strange and unaccountable to you, but I could not sit down to tell you only that I was in despair of ever being able to do anything in London, as was the fact for a long time. I never will think or talk upon the subject again. It was a year such as I did not think it possible I could have outlived, and the very recollection of it puts me into the horrors.[8]

Banim was eager to assist him in any way he could and called on Griffin to tell him that Maginn, who was then writing for *Blackwood's*, had offered to introduce Gerald (whom he had never met) to Jerdan, the editor of the *Literary Gazette*. Banim also asked him to dine at his house in order to meet Maginn and other literary people who might have been of help to him. Griffin declined the invitations, because (he writes to William) of the state of his clothes. Banim did not take offence at the refusal but called at Griffin's lodgings and left a note to say that he would be happy to introduce Gerald to these useful literary contacts whenever he chose to meet them. He also offered Gerald introductions to Moore and Campbell, but these offers too were rejected. 'I do not wish to know anyone until I have done something to substantiate my pretensions to such acquaintance, and to preserve it, if I can do so,' writes the purposefully independent Gerald to William on March 31, 1824.

From having been a frequent visitor to the Banim household he now began to neglect his friend entirely. Banim clearly tried very hard not merely to keep in touch with the younger man but also to buttress his self-esteem by inviting his views on his own recent writings. Griffin explains in a letter to his brother that he has been so busy looking for lodgings and for work that he neglected to call on Banim when the latter had invited him to comment on a recent work of his. When he did call on Banim, he found that the composition had already been despatched and he felt that Banim's manner to him had cooled on account of his neglect. He now disappeared from everyone's view for a time. He hid himself away in what he called 'a mouse-hole' of a lodging near St Paul's, did not write to his family, did not see Banim or any other friend, and was often in genuine want. Banim sought him out but Griffin was not at home when his friend arrived at his wretched lodgings. Banim, appalled by the evidences of his fellow-writer's destitution, called a second time and again failed to find his young countryman at home. He then wrote in a most friendly fashion, offering financial assistance until Griffin's fortunes should mend a little. Griffin seems to have resented this offer of help. Daniel's brotherly account in the *Life* suggests a sharp rejection of the intrusion into his pathetic privacy:

> It is sufficient to say that the offer was rejected with a degree of heat and sharpness which showed that he (Banim) had not succeeded in lulling the dangerous feeling to which I have alluded, and that his good-natured attempt proved so completely abortive, that there was evidently no use in pursuing the matter further. The friends did not meet again for some time, and the circumstance occasioned a degree of estrangement which it was not easy to repair.[9]

This early break with Banim was to create a touchiness in their relationship that was to result in a more serious estrangement several years later, when Banim again tried to come to Griffin's assistance.

GRIFFIN'S WORK FOR THE LONDON JOURNALS

Finding specimens of Griffin's work for the London journals proved a difficult and time-consuming task. The only real guide in this matter is to be found in the stray remarks contained in the letters and fragments of letters included by Daniel in the *Life*. The letters themselves are often undated, with names excised, and fragments of letters are always undated. Daniel's use of the letters is discursive and unsystematic. Added to these preliminary obstacles are the more serious ones provided by Griffin's own fondness for pseudonyms and anonymity, a fondness which clearly reflects those devious nuances of his character which are otherwise manifested in his disagreements with friends and his circuitous relationships with editors from whom he frequently concealed his real name. A letter to his parents in America, dated February 1, 1826, and addressed from 15 Paddington Street, Regent's Park, shows that even his own family were puzzled and unable to identify his pieces: 'Mary Anne asks me to give her some mark by which she may know my papers, but I cannot furnish one. I put five hundred different signatures; often none whatever, as I would not have acquaintances here recognise all I chose to write.'[10] This is at once tantalising and revealing. Much of what he wrote for the journals at this time was of an ephemeral character and failed to measure up to the lofty standards of excellence he set himself in his serious writing. Frivolity never came easily to him and he clearly despised much of what he churned out for the popular papers of the day.

The Literary Gazette

The first clear lead is given by Daniel when he says that the poem *I Am Alone*, which appeared in the *Literary Gazette* of July 3, 1824, signed with the pseudonym 'Oscar', was written by Gerald to express his intense feelings of isolation at this time. This enables us to trace what seems to have been the first series of articles which he managed to sell. This is the series of nine pieces indexed in the *Literary Gazette* under the general title *Horae Monomienses*, which appeared at fortnightly and some- times monthly intervals, beginning on June 5, 1824, over the suitably Celtic alias 'Oscar'.[11] Not surprisingly, this first journal- istic foray is based on his knowledge of Irish customs and consists mainly of pieces in which the Irish and their practices are explained and interpreted to an English audience. The pre- vailing tone is that of the early Anglo-Irish writer conscious of the alien quality of what he is describing and of the strange Irish-English in which it is often rendered. It is a tone already found in the explanatory notes to Maria Edgeworth's hugely popular *Castle Rackrent*. In the first piece, *Irish Satire*, Griffin writes: 'I have been enabled to procure some instances which are current amongst the peasantry of the South of Ireland, in their vernacular tongue; and I shall venture to subjoin a few, almost literally rendered into English.' This linguistic self- consciousness, this feeling that he must offer himself as inter- preter of a Gaelic-speaking people and of an emergent Anglo- Irish, is to be characteristic of all of Griffin's prose output and is to affect his writing to the very end. He manages, in general, to avoid any note of condescension to his material, always writing with genuine feeling for the plight of the people he describes. There is a note of real sincerity about his account of the lamenting mother in Letter ii, *The Irish Funeral Cry*.

The third of the sketches, *St Sinon's Isle*, is superficially an account of a boat trip to the island Scattery, near Kilrush in County Clare. Its real interest lies in the way in which Griffin seizes the opportunity to depict various kinds of Irish character in the course of the slight adventure. He is himself the mildly sardonic observer, Master Oscar. He has with him a Miss O'Shaughnessy, whose name proves difficult to pronounce, and 'her sister's husband's cousin, Mr Thady O'Histin, of Killimicat, a young gentleman who had been once to London, and since his return affected to despise everything Hibernian'. Mr Thady O'Histin has an exaggerated idea of his own importance and has 'cast away his vulgar family name, or rather qualified it, by writing Mr Thaddeus Hastings on his cards, to the great vexation of his guardian and uncle, an old Histin, who was proud of the name'. Thady O'Histin is made the butt of the piece – he lies languidly on the bench 'in affected *ennui*' while the others admire the beauties of the scenery and when they exclaim over the ruins and the churches Thady 'began to talk of Westminster Abbey and Stonehenge'. Griffin was to retain his interest in depicting this kind of absurdly Anglicised Irish snobbery, and characters of the Thady O'Histin variety were to recur in his stories – one thinks, for example, of the absurd Mr O'Neil in *The Half-Sir* and of Mr Houlahan in Chapter 39 of *The Collegians* who 'thought it *genteel* not to know Irish' and drew down upon his snobbish affectation the wrath of the plain-spoken Dan Dawley.

Others of the sketches also contain hints of the writer's future development. Letter v, *The Dispensary – Village Literature*, is full of the sort of material which was to go into later works such as *The Rivals* and *Adventures of an Irish Giant*. It is a mixture of rural comedy and linguistic *brio* of the kind depicted in the hedge-school scene in Chapter 7 of *The Rivals*. Brief as it is, the sketch bubbles with life – it has in it dispensary doctors, smooth-tongued patients in search of Latin-filled prescriptions, village poets and a village priest who condemns contemporary poetry in a manner worthy of Mr Lenigan's classical assistant in *The Rivals*:

'Tisn't any fine, classical poetry we see ye about writing; sweet, neat lines, such as – there he is – Palemon and Daphnis used to make in

Horace long ago. No; these times are gone by. We have nothing now but *nugae canorae*, as Homer says. Oh! if Tityrus or Virgil were to rise out of their graves, and see such verses coming after them, I wonder what would they say to it? Sorrow a bit, if they would n't be ashamed they ever printed a line, or handled a pen and paper. *Avenis cera junctis tu indocte cum in triviis*, etc. as Meliboeus says; as much as to say, 'You illiterate fellow, you go for to sing on the *boreens*, when you should be closing brogues with wax.'[12]

'Oscar' turns into a cleverly employed *persona* who serves both to convey to the English reader the humours of Irish life and to indicate the ambiguity of Irish attitudes to things English. Letter VII contains an amusing account of how the news of the death of a royal personage gets through too late to an Irish village determined to demonstrate its loyalty by sharing in the national grief. As a result of the delay in communications, the shops which plan to put up their shutters as a sign of respect do so at quite the wrong time; the whole exercise in public loyalty is wrong-footed and: 'That day, while all the rest of the British Empire mourned, the city of — and her dependancies waxed merry and busy; and when the cloud had passed from the world beside, they had at last their time of exclusive sorrow.'[13] The series of sketches closes with an account of a Rockite attack on a gentleman's farm-house. Mr Peppard of Cappa House, with his sons, defends his property gallantly against attack and the incident is made to reflect credit on the defenders. The Rockites are seen as pathetically misguided and disorganised felons. This would seem to bear out Ethel Mannin's contention, in *Two Studies in Integrity*, that Griffin was, in politics, a middle-class conservative, but it must be borne in mind that the *Literary Gazette* would not have accepted a piece written to glorify agrarian outrage and also that there is plenty of evidence in Griffin's later fiction that he had a genuinely sympathetic understanding of the root causes of such violence. All in all, this first series of journalistic sketches is most interesting in showing us the writer's first efforts at handling what was to be, at a later stage, the staple material of his stories. While he was still vainly trying to peddle his plays, still convinced that his literary future lay in the drama, his workaday pen was turning out the first examples of his characteristic prose.

The News of Literature and Fashion

Griffin began to write regularly for this London periodical in 1825. He describes in an interesting letter to his parents how he wrote some sketches of London life and sent them anonymously to the editor, offering to contribute to the paper without payment. To his surprise, the editor took the sketches and paid handsomely for them. These pieces were not signed and for a long time Griffin refused to reveal his identity to the editor, Walker, who seems to have tried hard to discover his coy contributor's name. Eventually Walker invited the anonymous writer to visit him at his country house and, after some hesitation, Griffin finally called on the Walkers at home. His account of this is revealing:

I went to his country house and found him there with his wife – a very elegant woman, and family; surrounded by harps, harpsicords, pianos, piazzas, gardens, in fact a perfect palace, within and without. He professed the highest admiration for me, for which I do not care one farthing; but that at first it led me to suspect he had some design of cheating me at the end; such is the way of the world; but I do so much for him now, that I have in some degree made myself necessary.[14]

In a subsequent letter to his parents he writes: 'Mr W— and I still get on very well together. He has given me the reviewing department of his paper, as well as the political and dramatic; so that here I have been made a critic almost before I became an author.'[15] All the letters he writes home at this time show Gerald's characteristic craving for anonymity as well as his curious mixture of arrogance and unease. It would clearly have been in his best interests to charm and flatter Mr Walker and his lady but, in a letter to William Griffin, he actually refers to Mrs Walker as 'a pleasing woman – no great shakes of a musician after all'. Again, although he is glad of the money coming to him from his work for the *News*, he is clearly suspicious of his editor. Walker's commendations serve only to implant in Gerald's touchy mind the notion that 'he has some design of cheating me at the end'. Ironically, these suspicions were to receive some confirmation later, as he writes to William on July 31, 1826 that the '*News of Literature* is dead and buried,

leaving me unpaid to some amount – enough to be disagree-
able'.[16]

A general distinction can be drawn between the work he did
for the *News* and the series of sketches, *Horae Monomienses*, in
the *Literary Gazette*. In the latter, as we have seen, Griffin was
producing sketches of a regional nature for an alien audience.
In the *News*, however, his function is quite different. He is here
playing the role of the fashionable London journalist and all
traces of his Irish nationality are erased. For a year or more he
becomes a regular theatrical reviewer, more familiar with the
performances of Fanny Kelly, Macready, Young and Kean than
with the Ireland he has left behind. That he was not entirely
happy in this role is clear from some of his letters. Daniel
quotes some of Gerald's own comments on his journalistic
endeavours: 'They are great trash, with however, a few novelties, and some passable writing – free and easy on my part you
will say. The editor tells me they are admirable, but he's a
quiz.'[17] And, again: 'By the rhymes I sometimes send you, you
may perceive I am putting myself in training for Warren's Jet
Blacking.'[18] The reference to Warren's Jet Blacking is a reminis-
cence of the rhyming jingles used to advertise this commodity
on the front pages of *The General Advertiser or Limerick Gazette*,
the paper for which Griffin had worked for a short time before
leaving home for London. The note is that of the serious literary
artist trapped by the need for money into writing advertising
jingles. He actually refers to his verses as 'crambo jingle'. He
seems, however, at this point to be grateful enough for the
money they bring in, which enables him to survive and get on
with his more serious work. It has proved possible to identify
a number of Griffin's contributions to the *News* with complete
certainty. As will be seen, he appended a variety of initials to
his pieces and sometimes published anonymously.

Sketches of Manners: Professed People

These are referred to by Griffin in a letter in which he describes
how he sent 'a couple of essays or sketches of London life, or
some trash of the kind anonymously' to the editor of the *News*.
This letter is undated but it contains a reference to the poem on

Liston which Griffin contributed to the *News* on June 25, 1825;
'I have just been scribbling off two hundred words of an epistle
to Liston on his return to London – poetry of course.'[19] The
letter, therefore, must have been written in early June or just
before and helps to trace the series of six sketches referred to
earlier in the same letter. The first appeared on February 19
and the last of the six on April 9. The writer's attitude to them
is summed up as follows:

I am furnishing him now with a regular series, of which he has had
six in number already. I generally get in from thirty shillings to two
pounds per week in this way, which, if it continues, is pleasant
enough, considering that it does not interfere with my other occupa-
tions.[20]

The pieces themselves bear out this judgement. They are
slight in texture, just mildly amusing comment of a chatty
nature on generalised subjects. Characterless as they generally
are, occasional points of detail help to identify them as Griffin's
work. The hit at the Lake poets and particularly at Wordsworth,
in Sketch No. 1, *Authors*, recalls the piece of bad verse in which
Griffin attacked these writers:

> Wordsworth, and Coleridge, and Landor, and Southey,
> Are stupid, and prosy, and frothy, and mouthy,
> Like a — and a — they sit side by side,
> True brotherly emblems of dullness and pride;
> From morning till night they sit staring and blinking,
> And striving to make people think they are thinking.
> Like four Irish parsons oppressed with the dumps,
> Or like my poor grandmother's pig in the mumps;
> Compared with such garbage the trash of A. Tennyson
> To me is a haunch of poetical venison;
> Or Bulwer – as deep as the sky in a lake,
> Till the mud at six inches reveals your mistake.[21]

There are occasional illustrative references of an Irish nature,
always made from an English standpoint. The brief, comical
account of the Irish bagpiper at the conclusion of Sketch
No. 4 and the closing lines of Sketch No. 6 are examples of
this, but the sketches generally depend upon Griffin's experience of the theatrical and literary world of the London of the
day.

Epistle to Mr Liston On His Return To London

This is a lengthy piece of fairly competent comic verse extolling the merits of the famous comedian and suggesting a considerable familiarity on the writer's part with the gossip of the green-rooms of the day. Griffin must have worn this particular mask with a certain amount of discomfort, one feels, bearing in mind his own very serious approach to the drama and his ambitions to reform the London stage. Not all of his contributions to the *News*, however, were of this frothy, ephemeral nature, as the following items demonstrate.

Hints For The Formation Of A New Musical Entertainment

Gerald's eldest brother and guardian, Dr William Griffin, arrived in London during the month of September 1826, to stay with Gerald in his 'neatly furnished apartments in Northumberland Street, Regent's Park'. William's account of his stay with Gerald is given *verbatim* in Chapter 7 of Daniel's *Life*. The whole chapter is invaluable, giving as it does a vivid impression of Gerald's working life at this time. Among the other interesting details supplied by William is a full account of his brother's contact with Arnold, the manager of the English Opera House. It seems that Gerald had written to Arnold suggesting that he should produce an entirely English opera. In illustration of what he meant he submitted a piece of his own, *The Noyades*. Arnold expressed courteous interest and, shortly after, brought out a piece called *Tarrare*. Griffin's own work, which had the alternative title *Love and Gratitude*, was eventually put on in 1828 and ran for twenty-nine nights. It was favourably reviewed in the *Literary Gazette* of July 19, 1828, and the acting and singing of Fanny Kelly in the leading role particularly commended. By then, of course, Griffin had long left the London scene to return to his brother's home in Limerick.

In the two essays on the subject in the *News*, he argues for the encouragement of a native, English school of opera. Gay's *Beggar's Opera* is advanced as the prototype of what he had in mind. Experiments made subsequently by 'Henry Fielding and Co.' have seemed to indicate that the English tongue is essentially unsuited to the operatic mode, but, the argument runs, it only requires the emergence of a writer of adequate talents to prove all the critics wrong by showing that the English language is indeed highly suitable for 'harmonious recitative'. The article contains some very perceptive comments on the nuances of language (that subject on which Griffin like all his Anglo-Irish successors is most sensitively self-conscious). He argues that the precise significance of Italian recitative must often escape a London audience incapable of grasping rapidly the full complexity of a foreign tongue. What he had to say in this connection is of particular interest in the light of his own subsequent development as a writer:

There is a greater charm in idiom than in language itself. A sentence spoken in his own provincial quaintness will reach the soul of a Scot sooner than all the pomp of the most finished eloquence, even admitting him to be perfectly capable of appreciating the latter. There is a nationality in this, and a nationality in which I should be very sorry not to participate.[22]

Although Griffin is here urging the use of English as a suitable language for opera, the force of conviction which informs the argument must surely derive from his own creative dilemma as an Irish writer searching for an identity and an idiom of his own. The second of the two articles on this topic discusses the failure of the opera *Tarrare*, which had been produced by Arnold in the interval, to measure up to the standards required. A long review of this opera, presumably by Griffin, had appeared in the *News* a week before. Both the review of August 20 and the essay of August 27 make it clear that this was an elaborate and ambitious production. The review details the absurd intricacies of the plot and, although it is not entirely antagonistic, faults the mixture of dialogue and recitative. The essay is firm in its view that *Tarrare* is not at all the sort of thing desiderated in the first article: 'It is continuous, sustained and uniform; but it has nothing of a prevailing English character, as it should have, from first to last.'[23] Griffin discusses the point again in a letter to one of his sisters and once more insists: 'I want to have purely English music, and characteristically English recitative,

instead of an adapted Italian one, which does not express
the same sensations in the same way as an English one
would.'[24]

He corresponded with Arnold on the subject and Arnold expressed keen interest in the discussion and willingness to consider works by Griffin for production at the English Opera
House. Banim was using his considerable influence with Arnold
on Gerald's behalf and, had he been a man of different temperament, a new career as librettist might have been open to
him. As William's account makes clear, however, the whole
thing foundered as a result of unnecessary misunderstandings
between Banim and Griffin and, once again, because of Griffin's
touchiness under obligation. William seems puzzled by his
younger brother's failure to grasp at the chance of making some
easy money:

> As he took no more than a fortnight to write one of these operas, and
> the payment was so liberal, one would have imagined, when his other
> literary labours paid him so badly in comparison, that he would have
> devoted his whole time to them, as long as the encouragement con-
> tinued. But, far from evincing any disposition to take advantage of
> Mr Arnold's favourable opinion of his abilities, there appeared an
> evident reluctance about him to send in a new one.[25]

Banim also seems to have resented Gerald's refusal about this
time to contribute a story to the O'Hara series which was prov-
ing so popular a part of his own fictional output. Gerald published *Holland-Tide* shortly afterwards and Banim suspected
that he had this collection of stories already prepared when he
turned down Banim's invitation. William insists that this had
nothing to do with the matter and that Gerald was, as always,
motivated by his ambition to succeed by entirely original effort
and not by attaching himself to an already established reputation. At any rate, the misunderstandings multiplied and
Griffin did not pursue the opportunity opened to him by the
acceptance of *The Noyades*.

The two articles on a native English opera strike an unusually
serious note by contrast with his earlier contributions to the
News. In their evident desire to increase the importance of the
verbal part of the performance they are clearly an extension of
Griffin's general dramatic ambitions. He wants to reform not

merely the drama but also the opera. The cannier Arnold was
understandably wary and wrote to Gerald:

I must be strongly tempted indeed by the poem, and the composition, before I would venture on so hazardous and losing a speculation . . . I am convinced it is by gradual and judicious advances alone
that the town will be ever brought to sanction it.[26]

Griffin appended to these two pieces the initials T.C., a puzzling choice as they are very close to the initials of his celebrated
contemporary, Thomas Crofton Croker, and Griffin was shortly
after this angered by reviewers who compared his first book,
Holland-Tide, to Croker's fairy-tales. Tracing the two opera
pieces over the initials T.C., however, has helped to uncover the
following very interesting contribution made by Griffin to the
News of Literature and Fashion over the same set of initials.

Sheridan And His Biographer

This, which appeared as the leading article in the *News* of
October 22, 1825, is most remarkably revealing of those limitations in Griffin's aesthetic outlook which were eventually to
ruin him as a writer of fiction. The article is, superficially, a
discussion of Thomas Moore's biography of Sheridan. In reality,
however, it becomes a debate on the topic of artistic morality
and the excesses of genius. The suggestion that the impulses of
a true genius are of a kind beyond the grasp or judgement of
ordinary mortals is firmly rejected, and Sheridan is attacked as
a man who displayed great wit in his writing but great selfishness, meanness and petty cunning in his life. It is suggested that
Sheridan intended Charles Surface in *The School for Scandal* as
'a favourable reflection of his own character' and Charles is then
roundly condemned as a thorough scoundrel. Sheridan's private
life is condemned, Sheridan's play is thoroughly misinterpreted,
his own character impugned, and the writer huffs and puffs his
angry way to a furious conclusion:

Genius indeed! what is it, that it should entitle its possessor to an
exemption from the rules of morality, and the commonest and most
essential of our social regulations? – What are those impulses for
which we are called upon to make so extensive an allowance? If they
are, necessarily, evil, – if genius must, necessarily, draw injustice,

meanness and selfishness in its train, (which it is a folly to suppose,) – then, I say, – let genius increase and multiply, but keep me far from the acquaintance or influence of its possessors.[27]

We are listening here, for the first time, to the Griffin who later wondered why his public preferred Hardress Cregan to Kyrle Daly, the Griffin who, gradually but inevitably, began to interfere with the artistic independence of his characters so that his stories would stay 'in the lines they ought to go in'. The severity of the attack upon Sheridan and the perverse confusion of the life with the work must have alarmed Walker, editor of the *News*, because he felt it necessary to attach a disclaimer to the article, pointing out the erroneous character of the argument. Walker did not go to the heart of the matter and take up the question of the fundamental wrong-headedness of Griffin's approach to *The School for Scandal*, but this point was exposed a month later in a letter to the editor.[28] This admirably sensible letter disposed of Griffin's old-fashioned strictures against the play by analysing Charles's true role in the comedy as a carefully conceived foil to his brother Joseph, the 'man of sentiment'. Sadly, one feels that the nauseating Joseph was closer to Griffin's concept of the good man than the rakish Charles could ever hope to be. We see in the article on *Sheridan And His Biographer* the rigid and disastrously oversimplified approach to artistic truth which was to play havoc with Griffin's own art less than ten years later.

Mary-Le-Bone Lyrics

Two of these, II and IV, were included in Griffin's *Poetical Works* and thus provided a lead to the whole series of eight which appeared in the *News* between September 10 and November 12, 1825.

The Lyrics are a series of frolicsome comic verses on matters of contemporary fashionable interest in the theatre and the town. They are of critical interest precisely because they are so unlike the work by which Griffin is generally remembered. In them we see this young Irishman, whose original aim was nothing less than the wholesale reform of the London stage and whose fame finally rests on his Irish regional fiction, entertaining

the town with frivolous comic verses on London trivia and the
gossip of the theatres whose decadence he deplored. It is indeed
intriguing to listen to the solemn author of *Gisippus* light-
heartedly commending Madame Vestris' legs. The pieces are, at
best, competently trivial but they spring from Griffin's regular
contact with the theatres in his capacity as reviewer of plays
and provide an insight into the rapid decline of his own theatrical ambitions. Daily contact with the London theatres of 1825
must have rapidly convinced him that there was little hope of
success for the sort of serious, moral play which he himself
liked to write. In June of that year he wrote to his brother,
William:

Plays are now out of fashion completely. Elliston advanced Banim
one hundred pounds on his tragedy, and yet is not bringing it out.
Stephens is at Drury Lane; Elliston is done up – 'peppered for this
world, I warrant;' and the management changes. But theatrical
affairs are wonderfully altered. No person of any respectability goes
to a play now. Even the pit of the Opera has been blackballed, and
the boxes of that house are the only places of this kind where people
of any fashion are to be found. Nobody knew anything of Banim till
he published his O'Hara Tales, which are becoming more and more
popular every day.[29]

To 'tales' he would soon have to turn in search of literary
success. When Fanny Kelly expressed interest in *Gisippus*
Griffin sent her four acts of the play which she read and commended. She even talked of the possibility of a production at
Drury Lane. Oddly, Griffin never sent her the fifth act, never
followed up this encouraging lead from one of the most celebrated actresses of the day. The explanation of his surprising
failure to do so may lie in his growing conviction that the contemporary stage was interested only in absurd spectacle and
trivial stunts. It would be absurd to lean too heavily on such
ephemera as the *Mary-le-Bone Lyrics* but they are nevertheless,
in their facetious way, Griffin's oblique farewell to his grandiose
theatrical ambitions.

THE LONDON PERIOD: SUMMARY

The importance of Griffin's three-year stay in London during his
formative years cannot be too strongly stressed. The wounds

inflicted on his sensibility by his sufferings at this time were
lasting ones and these years were to prove decisive in shaping
his mature development. It is tantalising to speculate about
what might have happened had his early experiences in London
been only slightly different, as they might well have been. Had
he managed to win with his lost play *Aguire* even the sort of
succès d'estime which Banim had gained with his *Damon and
Pythias* a little earlier, his entire life might have taken a very
different direction. His was a nature which was compounded
of an uneasy balance between ardour and reserve. Encouragement and approval at the right time could have served to propel
him along a path very different from the one he eventually
travelled. The crude and thoughtless rejection of his first play
by Macready and the dire miseries of his first year alone in
London killed a core of warmth in his creative nature and dis-
torted his entire development.

What emerges most clearly from a study of the journalistic
work he did at this time is his energy, variety and inventiveness.
He despised much of what he did for the *News* but, reading
through the issues for the whole year of 1825, one is struck by
his ceaseless activity and the range of his interests: comic verse;
reviews of books and of plays; articles on opera; essays of a
regional or polite character on a wide range of topics – he was
ceaselessly active and always at least competent. He started
writing for the *News* in the belief that he could at least do as
well at that sort of thing as the contemporary contributors to
the journal, a tiny arrogance which events justified. Daily
experience of the London stage at a period rich in great actors
but poor in great drama must gradually have convinced him
that his early dramatic ambitions were irrelevant to the place
and the time. His letters and his theatrical reviews reveal his
disgust at the gimmickry and contrivances of the big theatres
and his hatred for the influence of self-centred actor-managers
intent on furthering their own careers. Like Banim, he turned
away from the stage to prose fiction and moved inevitably in
the direction of regional realism, an area already explored and
popularised by Maria Edgeworth, Scott and Banim.

It is clear that, for a time, he must have come very close to
despair. He underwent some crisis of religious belief during these

years, on which we now have no precise information (he mentions it in a letter of April 22, 1827 to Banim).[30] All that was most negative in his nature came unhappily into the ascendant at the expense of the very considerable qualities of warmth, ardour and geniality which he undoubtedly possessed. Even the poverty of his eventual literary aesthetic, the dreadful moralistic narrowness which finally killed the writer in him, may not unreasonably be traced to this period. If only he could have poured his considerable literary gifts forth in successful work and won acclaim by it, he might have fought his way out of the moral blinkers imposed on him by his upbringing and his lack of formal education. If the writer in him had been allowed to spread his wings in the sun of public approval for a time at this important early stage, the London literary world might have seemed a more attractive place and he might have won through to some of the confident geniality of a Thomas Moore or a William Maginn. In studying this London stage of his career one is conscious always of his genuinely intense desire to write, of his almost feverish search for his proper *métier* as a writer, of his boundless energy which enabled him to cope with depressing quantities of dreary hack-work and of his violent swinging between an ardent confidence and a cynical despair.

The *News of Literature and Fashion* ceased publication in 1826. It was about this time that Griffin began to interest himself in writing a collection of Irish stories. In a letter to his family he asks them to help by supplying him with suitable anecdotes:

I am working up my recollections to furnish a book which I shall call 'Munster Anecdotes', a good title, with illustrations, etc. I have even had it announced in the *Literary Gazette* – rather too soon, for I can do nothing with it just now. My anecdotes are all short stories, illustrative of manners and scenery precisely as they stand in the south of Ireland, never daring to travel out of perfect and easy probability. Could you not send me materials for a few short tales, laying the scene about the sea-coast – Kilkee? novelty at least. Reality you know is all the rage now.[31]

Constant pressure of work made it very difficult for Gerald to press on with his stories:

Every moment brings something with it of the most pressing necessity. Besides my poor neglected anecdotes, which cry out unto me from the depths of a large table drawer, I have a three volume novel to correct in manuscript, concerning which I am sorely plagued – the author, who by the way gets £300 for it, is constantly worrying me to have it done. Then, jogging about to the newspapers, and then W—, from whom I have just now got a parcel of books to review; so that, as L— would phrase it, I can scarcely allow my ogles a blink at snooze time.[32]

The death of the *News* must have left him with a great deal more spare time for his own work and, with William urging him on, he completed the volume towards the end of 1826. William gives the following account of this:

Most of the tales in Holland-Tide were written in an inconceivably short space of time (not more than two or three months) before their publication, and entirely at my constant urging, and I can testify, from the difficulty I had in inducing him to make the effort at all, how very diffident and doubtful he was of success. I do not mean that he exactly underrated his own powers, but I believe he did not think that his engagements with the periodicals, which he could not give up, would allow him sufficient time and consideration to attain the success he was ambitious of, in a regular work of fiction.[33]

When he finished the book he offered it to Simpkin and Marshall who purchased the copyright for £70. Then, evidently feeling that this success had given him a foothold in the literary world, and at the insistence of his brother William who feared for his health, Gerald left London at the beginning of 1827 and returned home with William to Ireland. He thus brought to an end the most painful and critical part of his early experience, a period during which something had died in him which would never again revive, a period also during which he had battled his way towards a definition of the sort of work he was to engage in from now to the end of his career. He was never again to settle in England, though he was to return there at intervals throughout his career, to visit his publishers and to research the subjects of his novels. His most celebrated novel, *The Collegians*, was to be completed in London and both *The Invasion* (1832) and *The Duke of Monmouth* (1836) called for extensive researches in London and other parts of England.

3

Early prose works: *Holland–Tide* and *Tales of the Munster Festivals*

As we have seen, Griffin, having begun with high hopes of
establishing himself as a dramatist, found his way to prose
fiction through his work on various London periodicals, and the
current interest in regional tales such as those of Scott and
Banim. His letters, as given in Chapters 6 and 7 of the *Life*,
fill out the picture for us. In particular, William Griffin's
account in Chapter 7 vividly indicates Gerald's fever of activity
during 1826. He was reviewing books and plays, writing articles,
composing librettos for the English Opera House and making a
start on his collection of short stories. These were to be realistic
and regional tales in the manner of some of his journalistic
pieces about Irish life. One of modern Ireland's most distinguished men of letters, Padraic Colum, has commended
Griffin's early work:

'Hollantide' [*sic*] was written when he was twenty-three, and 'Tales
of the Munster Festivals' before he was twenty-five. These two
volumes would make a creditable introduction to a series of powerful
novels – they are on the level, for instance, with Thomas Hardy's
early books.[1]

Holland-Tide

This comparison with the early Hardy is reasonably accurate.
Holland-Tide and *Tales of the Munster Festivals* are not unlike
the Hardy of, say, *Desperate Remedies*, the Hardy of melodramatic confrontations and improbable contrivances. Griffin
shares Hardy's fondness for near-miss situations (for example,
Dorgan's narrow escape from hanging in *Card Drawing* and
Eugene Hamond's almost-marriage to Emily in *The Half-Sir*).

37

Like Hardy's, his early stories are marred by improbabilities.
Simple stereotypes in the realm of character are susceptible to
manipulation only by coincidences, lost letters, thunderstorms,
dreams, mysterious strangers and magic. The stories in *Holland-
Tide* abound in 'dramatic' confrontations (the scene between
Katharine Fitzmaurice and her father in *The Aylmers of Bally-
Aylmer*, for example) and well-known dramatic situations from
Shakespeare's plays tend to loom harmfully in the background
(for example, the scene in *The Aylmers of Bally-Aylmer* when
William Aylmer, Hamlet-like, confronts the ghost of his father).
The trial scene with which this story concludes, where Robert
Aylmer, who has been thought to be dead, returns to clear his
name and to exonerate his old friend Fitzmaurice from a murder
charge, is lurid melodrama. Indeed, Griffin seems conscious of
the need to cool the atmosphere a little by making the affair the
subject of jest among the lawyers in the courtroom:

'This beats the witch of Endor hollow,' said the crown lawyer, as he
threw his brief to the solicitor; 'your lordship may take place among
the cabalists of Domdaniel, after this.'
    Several other equally admirable witticisms passed among the
junior counsel on the back benches; such as that his lordship was a
clever resurrection-man – that he had given a *grave* turn to the
proceedings – that it was a dead-letter affair, with various inflictions
of a similar nature, which we grieve to say our slippery memory will
not enable us to lay before the reader.[2]

One regrets that Griffin did not more often give way to even this
kind of heavy-handed facetiousness – the melodrama is, all too
often, served quite straight.
    The diction employed in these early narrations is an alarm-
ingly periphrastic one, heavily larded with pseudo-Augustan
circumlocutions. Here is young Robert Aylmer setting out on
his journey to his guardian's home:

All traces of cultivation had not yet disappeared – the hardy potato,
in all its varieties of cup, white-eye, English red, kidney, London
lady, black bull, rattle, early American apple, white potato etc., etc.,
etc., diversified the ungrateful plain, with several plots or gardens of
variegated bloom, and filled the air with sweetness. The young
gentleman's pair of velocipedes, however, were so vigorous in the
execution of the trust confided to them, as to quickly place him
beyond the influence of these outskirts of cultivation.[3]

This distressing style is combined with the Irish regional writer's inevitable obligation to explain the oddities of regional customs and behaviour to an English public. It would be quite unfair to Griffin to suggest that he condescends to his material at any point. He does not, but at this point (and, perhaps, throughout his career) he works in two kinds of prose, the first this clumsily artificial 'grand' style which leads him into regrettable coyness and unfunny asides, and the other the homely style of his peasant characters with which he is much more successful. Edith Somerville was quick to remark this aspect of Griffin's writing:

The peasants are treated with simplicity: their language is not devoid of dignity, even sometimes of poetry; their characters, with the inevitable exception of the heroine, are more truly felt . . . It was the convention of Griffin's period that the higher the birth the taller the talk.[4]

More recently, Donald Davie has noted Griffin's stylistic dichotomy:

In *The Collegians*, as in many of Scott's novels, there is a yawning gulf between the vitality of the peasant's brogue and the frigidity of the more genteel dialogue. In Griffin, indeed, the gulf is far wider than ever it is in Scott. And in the same way, the descriptive writing is more florid and turgid than Scott's.[5]

In view of his obvious pleasure in the gaieties of Anglo-Irish, it is reasonable to suggest that, had his career developed differently and had he lived longer, Griffin might have won his way to a personal narrative style of an effective kind. Occasionally the writer's compassionate involvement with his characters appears with unusual clarity, as for example when he comments on the practice of the law in Irish courts. One such passage is to be found in *Holland-Tide* where Griffin inveighs against the freedom given to Crown lawyers to traduce the character of an accused man without allowing him the right of reply:

When we look at this fatal engine, which the law allows only to the accusing party, and consider that it is most frequently directed against some poor wretch who is not even acquainted with the language in which he is thus traduced in his own hearing, and consequently cannot avail himself of his privilege (!!) of reply, we may, perhaps, perceive why it is that persons once placed in the dock make their exit more frequently through the back than the front entrance,

why ropemakers thrive at a certain season, why the hangman can
endow his daughter so handsomely, and why the science of anatomy
is so attainable, and so practically understood in Ireland.[6]

Thomas Flanagan, commenting on this chapter, says:

we realize that this is the most alert eye which had yet looked upon
the Irish scene. Maria Edgeworth would never have used a court of
justice to explain why 'ropemakers thrive at a certain season, why
the hangman can endow his daughter so handsomely, and why the
science of anatomy is so attainable, and so practically understood in
Ireland'.[7]

It is certainly true that Griffin's prose loses much of its clumsiness when he engages in direct description of the Irish social
scene, and this is equally true of the change in his style when he
applies himself to descriptions of landscapes familiar to him
from childhood. We retain from his pages a memory of vividly
depicted places, of wide stretches of harsh, lonely bogland, of
mountains where law cannot reach and steep cliffs where
smugglers ply their profitable but risky business.

The most effective story in *Holland-Tide* is probably *The
Brown Man*, an effective piece of rustic Grand Guignol the
brevity of which preserves it from the structural defects of the
longer stories. In these the writer's control of the structure of
his tales is generally poor. He frequently interrupts the line of his
narrative to fill in some necessary part of the plot and he never
hesitates to break off to allow a character to tell a story whether
it happens to be relevant or not. The result is that it is easy to
lose the thread of the main story in catching up with the
clumsily inserted sub-plots. The writer frequently intrudes into
the narrative with coy comments on the habits of 'the fair sex'
or explanatory remarks addressed to the 'gentle London
reader'. Character is never explored. It is assumed that all young
ladies are virtuous, dutiful and proper and all young gentlemen
gallant, faithful and industrious except when they are led astray
by equally stereotyped villains. Such interest as the tales
possess consists in their presentation of a convincing landscape
and of glimpses of unfamiliar rural practices, such as the
touching of the corpse in *The Hand and Word*. Scott sums up
these aspects of Griffin's fiction in an extended comment on
Tales of the Munster Festivals:

The *Tales* are admirable. But they have one fault, that the crisis is in more cases than one protracted after a keen interest has been excited, to explain and to resume parts of the story which should have been told before. Scenes of mere amusement are often introduced betwixt the crisis of the plot and the final catastrophe. This is impolitic. But the scenes and characters are traced by a firm, bold and true pencil, and my very criticism shows that the catastrophe is interesting – otherwise who would care for its being interrupted?[8]

Tales of the Munster Festivals

The second volume of stories, published in 1827 under the title *Tales of the Munster Festivals*, contains three sizeable tales, *Card Drawing*, *The Half-Sir* and *Suil Dhuv the Coiner*. It shows a genuine improvement in many respects over the earlier book, *Holland-Tide*, and is of considerable interest both in regard to Griffin's literary development and the light it throws on his own mental make-up. The Introduction is extremely interesting as it shows Griffin speculating about the aims which are proper to an Irish novelist. He sets going an imaginary discussion between the writer and an 'old gentleman' in which he shows a considerable degree of sophistication in his attitude to his task as a novelist. When the narrator suggests to the old man that an Irish novelist 'might furnish the statesman and the legislator with an index to the dispositions and habits of the people he was to govern, and who were too distant for personal inquiry or observation',[9] the suggestion is mockingly rejected by his listener with the gibe that the narrator is like the music-master in Molière who attributed all evils to a want of the general diffusion of musical knowledge:

You would, I suppose, have a typhus fever, or a scarcity of potatoes, remedied by a smart tale, while you would knock a general insurrection on the head, with a romance in three volumes![10]

Bitterness and national resentment are close to the surface here and break through again when the old man continues: 'I am one of those who think that ruined people stand in need of a more potent restorative than an old wife's story.'[11] The narrator, however, fights back:

'You would have them write then,' said I, 'on the plan of some American novelists, who take care to construct their narrative, so as that they may be enabled to Jonathanize all the virtues, while all the villains of the tale shall be either Indians or Englishmen. For my part, I believe, and am proud to say it, the great majority of my country-men are far superior to that narrow-minded, national conceit which cannot relish a strong truth (even admitting it to be over-seasoned for the sake of *effect*), and which would prefer idle flattery to instruc-tion.[12]

Clearly, Griffin's London experiences which had so embittered him in some respects had also had the more positive and bene-ficial effect of providing him with a measure of detachment on Irish issues. The exchange here between the narrator and the old man is a debate conducted between the two halves of Griffin's sympathies and recalls his adoption of contrasting *personae* in the course of his journalistic sketches for the London papers. The alternation in his view of Irish affairs between a cultivated cosmopolitan detachment and an ardently involved enthusiasm has already been remarked.[13] The discussion now continues with a long exhortation from the old man which is of particular interest in view of Griffin's eventual development. He admonishes the writer to 'deal fairly with us. Give us our lights, if you will not overlook our shadows.'[14] He then launches into a highly emotional and sentimental account of the Irish past. The writer, if he finds the realistic depiction of contemporary Ireland a 'milk and water' business, should turn to 'the Ireland that was'. This dead Ireland is then lavishly praised in a highly rhetorical manner which evokes the scorn of the listening novelist:

'This leaves Jenkinson and the cosmogony far in the distance,' said I in my own mind, surveying my companion with a certain in-voluntary feeling of suspicion which I have entertained towards very learned talkers ever since I read Goldsmith's tale.[15]

The whole exchange demonstrates clearly that at this point in his development Griffin was well on the way to forming a really mature and fruitful attitude to his work as an Irish, expatriate novelist. The two extremes of sentimental praise and un-comprehending condemnation are rejected and the writer plumps for realistic depiction of the existing actuality. The sad irony which strikes one is that, in the event, Griffin was finally to lose the artistic detachment which he so clearly displays here and to

1 Gerald Griffin in 1830

2　Lydia Fisher

fall into the precise error enunciated in the old man's long final speech. It is in a dead Ireland that Griffin took refuge in his historical novel, *The Invasion* (1832). His eventual failure to develop a satisfactory aesthetic is all the more regrettable in the light of the clear evidence that he was already well on the way to doing so in his early twenties.

Two of the stories in *Tales of the Munster Festivals* (*Card Drawing* and *Suil Dhuv the Coiner*) are of the kind already made familiar in *Holland-Tide*. They are melodramatic, regional stories frequently spoilt by clumsily contrived plots, sometimes redeemed by vivid depictions of scenery or local conditions. Early in *Card Drawing* we are given the following hint of an aspect of the writer's practice which was to prove damaging to his style: 'But as the reader may observe throughout these tales, an ambition to render them almost as analogous to the drama as Fielding rendered his to the epic, (a circumstance in which the public taste seems, fortunately, to coincide with our inclination), we shall allow our hero to introduce himself.'[16] This histrionic inclination in the writer, this tendency to think in terms of 'strong' scenes of a 'dramatic' kind, was to persist. Later, he was to say of a scene in *The Collegians*: 'What a deal I would give to see Edmund Kean in that scene of Hardress Cregan, at the party, just before his arrest, while he is endeavouring to do politeness to the ladies, while the horrid warning voice is in his ear.'[17] As Padraic Colum points out, this sometimes led to impressive scenes but more often to a distortion of the story. There is, in this connection, an interesting note attached to the 1842 edition of the *Tales*. This does not appear in the first edition of 1827 and was presumably written by Daniel Griffin. It is attached to the second story, *The Half-Sir*, and refers directly to the mixture of narrative and drama in Griffin's work:

The plot of the foregoing tale is identical with that of a drama, in two acts, sent by the writer to Mr Arnold, late of the English Opera House. Subsequent occurrences induced the author to relinquish the desire of seeking an introduction to the public through the medium of the stage, notwithstanding the kind and pressing instances of the gentleman just named. The incidents of the tale are, so far as the writer is aware, entirely imaginary, but the manner in which they are treated still bears a strong impression of the mould in which they

were originally cast, and it is probable that what might have aided
their effect in scenic representation, has a directly opposite effect in
a performance intended solely for the calm and quiet consideration of
the parlour fire-side.[18]

Card Drawing is a simple, melodramatic tale of a sailor
wrongly accused of murder and rescued in the nick of time by
the repentance of the real murderer, but, in the course of it,
Griffin brings together a group of a kind we shall encounter in
his novels again. The forces of law and respectability are
represented by the Coroner, the priest and Dr Mahony. The real
murderer, Kinchela, with his wild companions, earns a precarious
living on the rocky shore, fishing and scavenging for 'barnocks'.
In between, we have the comical Mr Madigan, an inn-keeper,
a Malaprop whose affected and absurd English is richly mocked.
The atmosphere of wild lawlessness is presented as the logical
outcome of appalling social conditions:

it might be safely conjectured that the common routine of Munster
cottage life and education would produce that recklessness of blood
and outrage among *any* people, with which it has of late years been
fashionable to charge the inhabitants of this quarter of Ireland – as *a
natural propensity.*[19]

Kinchela's mother commonly addresses him in the Irish language and has a kind of simple, uncomplicated honesty which
distinguishes her from the silly and pretentious Madigan. Altogether, we are being presented with an accurate picture of a
society struggling to express itself in an emergent language,
struggling to come to terms with an alien code of justice – it is
a world which Synge would have found familiar and enthralling.
The writing, on the whole, is more direct and uncomplicated
than in the earlier volume, though *Suil Dhuv the Coiner* does,
perhaps, revert to the stylistic and structural clumsiness of the
longer stories of *Holland-Tide*.

The story in this volume which is of particular interest for the
student of Griffin is *The Half-Sir*. The figure which should command our particular attention here is that of Eugene Hamond.
What one remarks, first of all, is that the character of Eugene
Hamond is depicted with an unusual depth of psychological
insight. Hamond is a young man of humble birth who is reared
and educated by a wealthy second cousin of his father and, by

his education and his guardian's wealth, granted a precarious place in a class to which he has not been born. He is the 'half-sir' of the title, caught between 'simplicity and refinement'. He is also a young man of morbidly sensitive temperament, quite unfitted for dealing with the snubs and gibes of the ignorant, wealthy boors like Mr O'Neil, the well-born snob whom he encounters when he calls on the lady of his choice, Emily Bury. Mr O'Neil, whose family is 'one of the best in Ireland', is an effective comic creation who is depicted as a being filled with mock humility about himself and arrogance about his family, constantly protesting that he himself is but the black sheep of his line:

'Why, bless you, Miss Bury, *I* have relations that wouldn't know me in the street! Simple as I sit here, there's not one o' my family that wouldn't be ashamed to be seen speaking to me in any public place. There are few besides me have that to say. We were met, eighteen or twenty of us, at my cousin Harry's in Kerry some months since, and, I protest to you, without any bragging, boasting, or vain-glory, I was the shabbiest and the poorest of the company. Would you believe that now?'

'I could hardly believe that you take occasion for vanity out of such a circumstance.'

'Vanity! my dear! – It's my pride and glory – and why not? Arn't my relations my own family?'[20]

This nincompoop condescends to Eugene Hamond whom he regards as 'one of the rabble-mechanic' but, for a time, Hamond's natural goodness and integrity enable him to withstand the social strains to which he is subjected.

As always when he treats of this kind of morbid sensitive, Griffin writes with unusual penetration. Witness, for example, the effective scene in Chapter 4 when Emily Bury sets out to entertain the company with a funny tale about Eugene's servant, Remmy O'Lone. Her narrative requires her to pronounce local names of places and objects with which she is not familiar and she appeals to Eugene for assistance:

'Hamond was telling me a still more curious anecdote about him. He was sent once to a fair in Munster, the fair of Hanna – Vanna – Shana – what was it, Hamond?'

'Shanagolden,' said Eugene, bowing and smiling.

'O yes, the fair of Shanagolden. His mistress wanted to purchase half a dozen mug – hog – pig – '

'*Piggins*, they were,' said Hamond in reply to her puzzled look, 'p-i-g-pig, g-i-n-s-gins, piggins,' spelling the word, to show how coolly and equably he took it. 'A kind of wooden vessel used for drinking the coagulated residuum of milk, called by the peasantry thick, or skimmed milk.'[21]

This scene, with Emily Bury's casual condescension combining with Hamond's tense restraint (vividly conveyed in his spelling of the peasant word 'piggins'), has the peculiar life which Griffin always manages to impart to this kind of encounter. Here he abandons the contrived stereotypes which normally contented him and writes with his finger firmly on the pulses of his characters. Hamond is, in fact, the first in a line of such characters, the predecessor of Hardress Cregan and also of Gisippus, hero of the only one of his dramas which Griffin allowed to survive.

The relationship between Hamond and his benefactor is extremely well done. The uncle:

was one of those selfishly generous beings who confer a favour for their own sakes alone – and while they mingle so much ungracious rudeness with their liberality, as to make it a pain, not a pleasure to the receiver, yet look for as warm and abundant a show of gratitude as if the gift were not entirely a selfish action.[22]

Eugene, shy and lonely, fails to provide his uncle with the facile gratitude he wants and so they remain apart until the very end of the uncle's life. Eugene's is a nature 'sensitive even to a perfectly morbid acuteness of perception' and, in order to make his way in society, he decides to suppress his nature completely, with disastrous results:

If Hamond's gentle embarrassment and absence of manner, rendered him a burthen to his companions before – his new demeanour – his strange familiarity – his queer embarrassed laugh – his ill-timed joke that made every body look serious – and his intrusive dogmatism of remark, absolutely astonished, frightened, and disgusted them. Having once convinced himself of the expediency of doing violence to his own feelings, he knew not where to stop, and on passing the boundary which his own heart prescribed to him, he trampled without discrimination, and, indeed, in absolute ignorance, upon those which custom and decency had marked out for his observance.[23]

In despair, he is about to retire from society when a chance kindness bestowed upon him by Emily Bury at a fashionable party causes him to resolve upon remaining in society with the

intention of wooing Emily. He is successful in his suit but when
she makes a cutting remark about his family in company he
reacts with predictable sensitivity and releases her from her
engagement. Subsequently, Griffin allows the line of the story
to depend upon the inevitable undelivered letter and the lovers
are finally brought together at the end only after a long series
of mishaps.

Hamond is made a symbol of a society in disarray, a society
whose social values have gone hopelessly awry. Here is the
revealing exchange between the Wren-boy and Mr Falahee with
which the story opens:

'Have you been at Mr Hamond's yet, lads?' inquired Mr Falahee.

'Aw! not we, Sir. It's always the way with the Wran to pay his
compliments to the real gentlemen first.'

'Why – ' said the worthy but flattered host, with an ill-suppressed
smile, 'Is not Mr Hamond a real gentleman?'

'No, please your honour, not a real, undoubted gentleman, that
way, all out.'

'I'm sure Castle Hamond is as fine a property as there is in the
barony.'

'O we don't mean to dispute that, sir. But himself, you see, he's
nothing. What is he but a bit of a half sir?'

'A what?' exclaimed the elder lady.

'A half sir, ma'am,' turning toward her with great respect, and
giving his forelock a drag which seemed to signify that had he got
such a thing as a hat on, he would have taken it off to her honour.

'What do you call a half sir?'

'A man that has not got any blood in him, ma'am.'

'A man that has got no blood in him!'

'Noan; any more than meself. A sort of a small gentleman, that
way, the singlings of a gentleman, as it were.'[24]

The Wren-boy is Mr O'Neil's counterpart at the opposite end
of the social scale and Griffin is here exploring social complexities which had already occupied Maria Edgeworth in *Castle
Rackrent* and *The Absentee* and were later to concern most of the
Anglo-Irish novelists. Lever's *Lord Kilgobbin*, Charlotte Mullen
of *The Real Charlotte*, the whole social scramble of George
Moore's *A Drama in Muslin*, come to mind in this connection.

On the personal level, the story gives a real insight into
Griffin's own mind and many of the later passages have the
ring of unwitting autobiography. When Hamond is about to

emigrate, Griffin provides a lengthy comment on the embarking passengers, which clearly reflects much of his own grim experience:

> They saw the young, acutely sensitive, and fine-principled enthusiast, whom the folly of friends, or the consciousness of merit forced abroad upon the world – shrinking in disgust and agony from the cruel reality which displaced the faëry splendours of his own fond imagination – or curbing his high spirit down to the mean and crawling uses of a hireling and time-server – bartering his youthful principle for bread – or, perhaps, sternly preserving it, and turning aside from the wonder – the scorn – and indifference of the world, to die in want and solitude, and hide his brilliant qualities of heart and mind in the gloom of a pauper's grave, unthought of, and unpitied.[25]

The writer's genuine involvement with certain aspects of his material lends him an unusual force and insight. The unhappy childhood experiences of Eugene Hamond and his subsequent social disasters engender in him a hatred of those who have scorned and condescended to him and the blighting effects of these experiences on his character are traced with real penetration. Later in the story, when Hamond is working at relieving the famine-stricken poor, his muddled motives are convincingly analysed:

> The more Hamond saw of the misery, and of the dispositions of the impoverished classes of his countrymen, the more that dislike of the wealthy and high-born, which had constituted the disease of his mind for many years, was irritated and increased – and (without seeking maliciously to detract from the merit of his benevolence) we might say, that the poor benefited nearly as much by his resentment to their superiors, as by his compassion for themselves.[26]

There is a genuine link here between Eugene's peculiarly motivated charity and his guardian's perverted benevolence. This provides a kind of moral coherence for the narrative which has previously been absent from Griffin's stories. *The Half-Sir* sounds for the first time notes which will be heard even more clearly in Griffin's next and most celebrated work, *The Collegians.*

4

The Collegians

Holland-Tide, completed towards the end of 1826, was accepted by Simpkin and Marshall, who paid Griffin £70 for the copyright. He left London for home on January 30, 1827 and arrived in Pallaskenry early in February. His homecoming was saddened by the death of his sister, Ellen, who passed away just before Gerald's arrival. Once home, he awaited the reviews of *Holland-Tide* with some anxiety. These were generally favourable though Griffin was evidently much upset by the review in the *Literary Gazette* which likened one of his stories to those of Thomas Crofton Croker. Daniel's account of this throws an interesting light on Gerald's passionate desire for what he saw as genuine originality:

It was not rage so much his countenance expressed, as an appearance of the most violent agony. He crumpled the paper in his hand, raised it high above his head, stamped violently, and almost dashed it to the earth in the excess of his feeling. 'Oh!' he said – 'oh!' with a prolonged, and deep, and painful emphasis on the word – 'this was just what I feared. I told — these tales were like Crofton Croker's.' I was perfectly astonished, and said, 'Why, what signifies it?' 'Oh!' said he again, 'you don't know the effect of these things. *Only think*,' he repeated, with the utmost vehemence, '*only think of being compared with Crofton Croker*.'[1]

As the reviews were generally favourable, however, he was encouraged to begin work on *Tales of the Munster Festivals* which he completed and published in the same year, 1827. This, his first three-volume prose work, was also fairly well received by the reviewers, who nevertheless remarked certain faults which they ascribed to haste on the writer's part. The result of this was that he delayed the commencement of his work on his next book, *The Collegians*, until late in 1828. A letter to his

father makes clear his response to the adverse criticisms of his
second work:

The critics frightened me so much when I published my first series of
the Festivals, that I found it very hard to please myself in the
second. I wrote half a volume of one thing and threw it by, and a
volume and a half of another and threw it by also; but the third time
(as they say in the Arabian Nights) I was more successful in satisfying
myself. Nevertheless, the delay threw me back several months, as it
was settled that my second series should appear about November,
and that month found me with only half the work written. Thus,
instead of being done with greater deliberation than before, as the
Aristarchuses advised, my present unfortunate tale has been actually
written *for the press*, and sent sheet after sheet to the printer according
as it was done. However, I am in no great uneasiness about it, as I
feel that it is a great improvement on the former at any rate.[2]

Daniel had joined him in London in November 1828, and was
lodging with him while Gerald completed *The Collegians*. His
account of this period makes it clear that Gerald was telling the
literal truth when he wrote to his father that the book was
written 'for the press':

Every morning almost, just as we were done breakfast, a knock came
to the door, and a messenger was shown in, saying, 'Printers want
more copy, sir.' The manuscript of the previous day was handed
forth, without revision, correction, or further ceremony, and he went
to work again to produce a further supply. The most singular part of
the business was, that he very seldom broke in upon his usual rule of
not writing after dinner; but every moment of next morning, up to
breakfast hour, was occupied in preparing as much matter as possible
before the dreaded printer's knock.[3]

In the light of what we know about Griffin's moral scrupulosity and its damaging effects on his work, this importunacy of
the printers and the speed of composition it imposed on him
may have been enormously to the book's advantage. This
seems even more probable in the light of his subsequent comments on the novel and his peculiar misgivings about its hero,
Hardress Cregan, to which reference will be made later. *The
Collegians* was to prove Griffin's most successful and enduring
work. It earned him £800 (which he sent to his parents in
America) and proved immensely popular in his own time and
throughout the nineteenth century. Literary fame is a chancy
business but the affectionate and enduring regard bestowed upon

this novel is of a kind which is rarely earned by a really insignificant work. *The Collegians* is, in fact, a novel of central importance in the Anglo-Irish literary tradition and also, in regard to Griffin himself, a remarkably revealing document. It will be the purpose of the present chapter to explore both these aspects of the book as fully as possible.

The novel was based on a celebrated murder case which had caught the public attention while Griffin was in his teens.[4] Early one morning towards the end of July 1819, the body of a young woman was washed ashore near Kilrush, County Clare. She was identified as Ellen Hanley, a girl of not quite sixteen years who had disappeared from the home of her uncle and guardian, John Connery, towards the end of June. John Scanlan, son of one of the leading county families, was arrested and brought to trial for the murder. A second arrest took place some months later when Stephen Sullivan, Scanlan's boatman, was captured and tried. Both men were hanged, Scanlan in March 1820 and Sullivan in the following July. Scanlan was defended by no less a figure than the Liberator, Daniel O'Connell, and his trial attracted enormous public interest. The prosecution charged that Scanlan had married or pretended to marry Ellen Hanley and that later, fearing the hostility of his family to his marriage with a peasant, he had brought about her death. O'Connell, in his defence, argued that the murder had really been committed by Stephen Sullivan and he evidently came near to swaying the jury, who first disagreed about their verdict but subsequently brought in a verdict of guilty.

It is sometimes asserted that Gerald Griffin actually reported the trial of Scanlan for a Limerick paper. There is no direct evidence of this. In March 1820 he would have been sixteen years old, which makes it unlikely. Furthermore, if he had reported this celebrated trial, Daniel would surely have mentioned it in the *Life*. He does, in fact, advert to Gerald's brief connection with McDonnel's paper, *The General Advertiser*, but makes no mention of the Scanlan trial. He later records that Gerald worked as a court reporter for a case involving Daniel O'Connell *after* Gerald's return from London in 1827 and it is possible that the amusing incident which took place then, in connection with O'Connell's glancing at Griffin's manuscript, may have given rise to the suggestion that Griffin had reported the earlier case.[5] The story goes that Gerald, bored perhaps by the legal matters going on around him, took time off from his duties as court reporter and began to scribble away furiously at some story of his own while the business of the court droned on. Daniel O'Connell, who is said to have greatly admired *The Collegians*, noticed the handsome young court clerk who seemed so absorbed in what he was writing and, during some pause in the proceedings, leaned over and picked up Griffin's papers, little knowing that he was in the presence of the author of the famous novel which he regarded so highly. It would have been entirely characteristic of Griffin to have retained his anonymity even in the presence of so famous an admirer.

Whether he reported the case or not, there is no doubt that it would have made a profound impression on the young Griffin, himself almost the same age as the unhappy victim. The brutal murder of the young peasant wife, instigated by the well-born Scanlan and carried out by his devoted henchman, Sullivan, was to prove, a decade after the event, the ideal framework for a novel in which Griffin vividly expresses both himself and the age in which he lived. This latter aspect of the novel, the social aspect, has been interestingly touched on by Thomas Flanagan who has shown in a lively and discerning analysis how Griffin used his story to depict many levels of the society of his time and to condemn powerfully one of those levels, that of the 'half-sirs' or squireens, the Hepton Connollys and Hyland Creaghs who hunt and drink and duel their way through the novel, themselves the most lawless symbols in a chaotic society:

The novel involves, eventually, the entire structure of provincial Irish society: the gentry, from the Chutes of Castle Chute to the Creaghs and Connollys and Cregans of Roaring Hall; middlemen like the Dalys, torn in their feelings between the Gaelic past and the Anglo-Irish present; the English of the Garrison: Leake, a physician, Gibson, the commandant of militia, Warner, the magistrate. Below these the peasants, the landless men, the shopkeepers of Limerick town, the horse traders of the Kerry mountains, the boatmen.[6]

The novel begins appropriately with an evocation of a vanished, pastoral innocence. Garryowen, 'Owen's Garden', is another Auburn from which the simple glories have now departed:

The days of Garryowen are gone, like those of ancient Erin; and the feats of her once formidable heroes are nothing more than a winter's evening tale. Owen is in his grave, and his garden looks dreary as a ruined church-yard. The greater number of his merry customers have followed him to a narrower play-ground, which, though not less crowded, affords less room for fun, and less opportunity for contention.[7]

The innocent Eily O'Connor is first introduced to us as part of this idyllic scene from the past. She is the daughter of Mihil O'Connor who conducts the business of a rope-walk in the neighbourhood and who comes to Owen's pleasure-garden to pass his leisure hours. Griffin has, as Flanagan notes, surrounded Eily with symbols of death: her father's trade is associated with hanging; the rope-walk is near a gallows green and near at hand are a pest-house, a coffin-maker's shop and a churchyard. Eily has received some education from her uncle, Father Edward, a parish priest who has been schooled at Salamanca. Her natural refinement and her extra schooling make her, for the purposes of the novel, a more feasible bride for Hardress Cregan although he will later find her peasant accent a sore trial. Like Tess Durbeyfield, Eily first encounters her lover at a dance during a village festival and, again like Tess, is shortly afterwards rescued from some persecutors by her lover. The opening of the novel is speedy and effective. Eily's disappearance from her father's house has been briskly contrived by the end of the second chapter.

We are then introduced at some length to Mr Daly and his family. They represent the emergent middle classes and Griffin is at some pains to define their place in society. Mr Daly himself is a 'middleman' and a strong farmer:

Opprobrious as the term 'middleman' has been rendered in our own time, it is certain that the original formation of the sept was both natural and beneficial. When the country was deserted by its gentry, a general promotion of one grade took place amongst those who remained at home. The farmers became gentlemen, and the labourers became farmers, the former assuming, together with the station and influence, the quick and honourable spirit, the love of pleasure, and the feudal authority which distinguished their aristocratic archetypes – while the humbler classes looked up to them for advice and assistance, with the same feeling of respect and of dependence which they

had once entertained for the actual proprietors of the soil. The covet-
ousness of landlords themselves, in selling leases to the highest bidder,
without any enquiry into his character or fortunes, first tended to
throw imputations on this respectable and useful body of men, which
in progress of time swelled into a popular outcry, and ended in an act
of the legislature for their gradual extirpation. There are few now in
that class as prosperous, or many as intelligent and high-principled,
as Mr Daly.[8]

Flanagan has noted some puzzling elements in the novelist's
presentation of the Daly household:

> The walls are crowded with prints – Hogarth's 'Roast Beef', Prince
> Eugene, Schomberg at the Boyne, Betterton playing Cato. There
> would be nothing improper in this, certainly, were it an English or an
> Ascendancy household. But the Dalys are Catholic and native Irish,
> and this makes their taste in decoration wildly inappropriate, for
> they have chosen to honor Hogarth's most robustly British scene, an
> English actor playing a Roman statesman, the ally of Marlborough,
> and, of all people, the Protestant mercenary who delivered Ireland to
> William of Orange. Perhaps the full weight of this incongruity needs,
> for its appreciation, some familiarity with Irish loyalties, but it
> borders on the grotesque.[9]

The 'incongruities' to which Flanagan points would, one feels,
be out of place if the society Griffin is depicting were a normal,
stable one. As Flanagan himself indicates, however, it is no such
thing. It is a society whose values are in turmoil and the various
levels of which are in the constant state of flux described in the
extract from *The Collegians* just quoted. The Daly family are
surely the fictional equivalent of the Griffin family itself with
Charles Daly in the part of Gerald's father, Patrick Griffin. The
novel is, as Thomas Flanagan indicates, 'set in the seventeen-
seventies, when Ireland was astir with the news of the Volun-
teers, of Grattan, of the first Catholic concessions'. Mr Daly is
a supporter of Henry Grattan and, therefore, by definition a
parliamentarian, a constitutionalist. He is also possessed of 'a
considerable number of works on Irish history – for which study
Mr Daly had a national predilection'. He has a son at the
Protestant university in Dublin and is clearly no revolutionary.
He is the necessarily confused though genial representative of
the emergent Irish Catholic middle class. From such a family of
strong farmers and budding professional men came Gerald

Griffin himself and, as has already been suggested in Chapter 1, he inherited much of the social caution of that class though he tempered his conservatism with compassion.

Mr Daly is, in turn, made to explain to us the social layers above his own and it is significant that he does so by means of two comic anecdotes carrying strong connotations of absurdity for the people involved. In the first of these we learn that Anne Chute is the step-daughter of the absurd little Tom Chute and the amazonian Hetty Trenchard, who has almost literally whipped her reluctant swain into matrimony in a splendid piece of Anglo-Irish comic bravura. The second mocking tale concerns Barny Cregan, father of Hardress. Barny, according to Mr Daly, has manifested his family pride 'in a manner that might make an Englishman smile' by erecting in the local churchyard an absurdly showy mausoleum adorned with a dubious Cregan crest. Thus, the Cregans have come up in the world fairly recently, Barny Cregan likes to get value for his money even in a graveyard and the Chute ménage has also provided the countryside with a modicum of amusement.

Attached to the Chute household as constant visitors and suitors are the squireens, Hyland Creagh and Hepton Connolly. Creagh is in his sixties but has been known in his younger days as a notorious duellist and member of the Hell-Fire Club. He has run through his own property and is now reduced to cadging food and wine from his wealthier friends. Hepton Connolly is another ruined half-sir who has 'retained enough of a once flourishing patrimony to enable him to keep a hunter, a racer and an insolent groom'. He depends on his family connections to keep him out of trouble with the authorities and, like Maria Edgeworth's Sir Murtagh Rackrent, has a great fondness for litigation in which he seems to engage for its own sake rather than for any profit which he might derive from it. These two, a combination of the dangerous and the ridiculous, are at once the root-cause of the decay of their society and the most tragic representation of that decay – they are at once source and symptom of the country's ruin. They are seen at their dangerous follies in Chapters 17 and 18 which depict the tragic death of Dalton the old huntsman and the near-murder of Hardress by Hyland Creagh.

In official control of the muddled Ireland of the novel are the
men of the Garrison: Dr Leake, Mr Warner, the magistrate and
Captain Gibson, the military man. These three who are regular
visitors at Castle Chute and are to be the eventual captors of
the luckless Hardress are depicted as being in but not of the
locality. Their position is always that of detached observers of
an alien society. When we first encounter Dr Leake, as a guest
at Castle Chute, he is depicted with effective irony as an antiquarian who is busy explaining to Captain Gibson the distinctions between the military methods of ancient Ireland and
modern Britain:

The rosy and red-coated Captain Gibson, who was a person of talent
and industry in his profession, was listening with much interest to
Doctor Lucas Leake, who possessed some little antiquarian skill in
Irish remains, and who was at this moment unfolding the difference
which existed between the tactics of King Lugh-Lamh-Fada, and
those issued from his late most gracious Majesty's War-Office;
between one of King Malachy's hobbilers and a life-guardsman;
between an English halberd and a stone-headed gai-bulg, and between his own commission of lieutenant and the Fear Comhlan
Caoguid of the Fion Eirin.[10]

Griffin does not always command this sort of forceful irony. It
surely arises here from his profound involvement with his
material. Dr Leake, explaining to a polite but uncomprehending
Captain Gibson the distinctions between ancient Ireland and
her modern conqueror, becomes a telling symbol of the mutual
incomprehension of seven centuries. Gibson himself, when taken
to the local races, plays the part of the visiting Englishman to
perfection. The scene is as vivid and entertaining as one by
Somerville and Ross:

Captain Gibson, who now approached them on foot, could not, with
the recollections of Ascot and Doncaster fresh in his mind, refrain
from a roar of laughter at almost every object he beheld, – at the
condition of the horses; the serious and important look of the riders;
the *Teniers* appearance of the whole course; the band, consisting
simply of a blind fiddler with a piece of *listing* about his waist and
another about his old hat; the self-importance of the stewards, Tim
Welsh the baker, and Batt Kennedy the poet or *janius* of the village,
as they went in a jog trot round the course, collecting shilling sub-
scriptions to the saddle from all who appeared on horseback.[11]

The novel abounds in vignettes of this sort, exposing the complex muddle of early nineteenth-century Irish society. A particularly vivid one is found towards the end of the novel when Mr Warner attempts to cross-examine the redoubtable Poll Naughten and her husband Philip. The entire chapter deserves the closest reading. At this point in the action, Hardress Cregan's servant, Danny Mann, who has actually killed Eily, has already been examined but has managed to give a series of evasive answers: 'His answers were all given in the true style of an Irish witness, seeming to evince the utmost frankness, and yet invariably leaving the querist in still greater perplexity than before he put the question.'[12] Mr Warner, irritated by Danny Mann's evasiveness, decides to examine his sister, Poll Naughten and her husband, Philip, separately in order to compare their stories. This causes Mrs Cregan intense anxiety on Hardress's behalf but her fears are, at this juncture, proved groundless. The reasons for this are expounded in a passage which would have found a sympathetic reader in the author of *The Playboy of the Western World:*

The peasantry of Ireland have, for centuries, been at war with the laws by which they are governed, and watch their operation in every instance with a jealous eye. Even guilt itself, however naturally atrocious, obtains a commiseration in their regard from the mere spirit of opposition to a system of government which they consider as unfriendly. There is scarcely a cottage in the south of Ireland where the very circumstance of legal denunciation would not afford even, to a murderer, a certain passport to concealment and protection. To the same cause may be traced, in all likelihood, the shrewdness of disguise, the closeness, the affected dulness, the assumed simplicity, and all the inimitable subtleties of evasion and of wile which an Irish peasant can display when he is made to undergo a scene of judicial scrutiny, and in which he will frequently display a degree of gladiatorial dexterity that would throw the spirit of Machiavelli into ecstacies.[13]

The termagant Poll copes more than adequately with Mr Warner's questions by a series of evasive, angry and highly amusing replies. Mr Warner gives her best at last: 'I'm afraid you are too many for me. What shall we do with this communicative person?' he said, turning to the other gentlemen. 'Remand her,' said Captain Gibson, whose face was purple with

suppressed laughter, 'and let us have the husband.'¹⁴ When
Philip Naughten is brought in his timid and deprecating manner
induces in Mr Warner the hope that this witness may prove
easier to handle than the furious Poll but he is in for yet another
shock. He is now treated to another variation on Irish duplicity,
this time the linguistic one:

'Now, we shall have something,' said Mr Warner, 'this fellow has
a more tractable eye. Your name is Philip Naughten, is it not?'
The man returned an answer in Irish, which the magistrate cut
short in the middle.
'Answer me in English, friend. We speak no Irish here. Is your
name Philip Naughten?'
'Tha wisha, vourneen – '
'Come – come – English – Swear him to know whether he does not
understand English. Can you speak English, fellow?'
'Not a word, plase your honour.'
A roar of laughter succeeded this escapade, to which the prisoner
listened with a wondering and stupid look. Addressing himself in
Irish to Mr Cregan, he appeared to make an explanatory speech
which was accompanied by a slight expression of indignation.
'What does the fellow say?' asked Mr Warner.
'Why,' said Cregan, with a smile, 'he says he will admit that he
could'nt be *hung in English before his face* – but he does not know
enough of the language to enable him to *tell his story* in English.'
'Well, then, I suppose we must have it in Irish. Mr Houlahan, will
you act as interpreter?'
The clerk who thought it *genteel* not to know Irish, bowed and
declared himself unqualified.
'Wisha, then,' said a gruff voice at a little distance, in a dark
corner of the room, 'it is'nt but what you had opportunities enough
of learning it. If you went in foreign parts, what would they say to
you, do you think, when you'd tell 'em you did'nt know the language
'o the counthry where you were born? You ought to be ashamed o'
yourself, so you ought.'
This speech, which proceeded from the unceremonious Dan Dawley,
produced some smiling at the expense of the euphuistic secretary,
after which the steward himself was sworn to discharge the duties of
the office in question.¹⁵

This scene is packed with the most interesting insights into
the variations of Irish evasiveness and social pretension. Mr
Houlahan, 'the clerk who thought it *genteel* not to know Irish',
is a cruelly accurate touch. The entire chapter shows Griffin at
his best because in it he brings to bear on the Irish scene he

knew so well his peculiarly penetrating, bifocal vision. He combines here the strengths of the talented native and the experienced expatriate. One is reminded of the powerful scene in *The Real Charlotte* in which Charlotte Mullen employs her knowledge of the Irish language to intimidate her tailor Dinny Lydon, who cannot be quite sure how much of his Irish conversation with his wife has been understood by the redoubtable Miss Mullen. It is such insights and the lively and vigorous scenes they produce which give the novel its impressive solidity as social commentary. As Flanagan puts it:

Griffin had not written a novel *about* Ireland; he had written an Irish novel. The Ireland of *The Collegians* is not presented to the reader as an object of sympathy or commiseration or indulgent humor. It simply exists. It exists in rich and exact detail; it is 'picturesque' and 'romantic', enchanted and accursed. But it is given to us in a work of art, not in a disguised tract. And even when the complexities and ironies of the novel went unnoticed, its moral feeling struck a responsive chord. Griffin was an acute moralist and one who lived within the same world of moral experience as did the majority of his countrymen.[16]

Added to this impressively solid foundation there is an interesting further dimension of melodramatic achievement in the depiction of the book's celebrated hero, Hardress Cregan, whose glamorous and excitable character takes us to the heart of the reasons for the novel's success and to the core also of Griffin's personal puzzle and paradox. Hardress is the most remarkable of a long series of Griffin 'sensitives', a group which includes Eugene Hamond of *The Half-Sir*, the Saxon Kenric in *The Invasion* and Gisippus, hero of the only play Griffin chose to preserve when he destroyed his papers. In these figures Griffin charted his personal dilemma and gave it artistic objectivity. The contention is not that the novels and the play are merely autobiographies in thin disguise but that, in these works, Griffin is exploring minds which he desperately needed to understand, minds subject to pressures all too familiar to the writer himself. That Griffin could create a Hardress Cregan and a Gisippus and yet fail to solve his own moral dilemma is a puzzle. The explanation must lie hidden in his life somewhere – it is a matter of unwritten biography. Perhaps it had something to do with the scarring of his psyche during his early struggles

in London. It must surely be linked with his brief loss of faith
during his early twenties and with his resumption of the practice
of his religion, matters which he discusses in a lengthy letter to
his fellow novelist, John Banim, in April of the year 1827.[17]
His frustrating love for a married woman, his Quaker friend
Lydia Fisher, may have had something to do with it – one can
now only conjecture. But whereas only conjecture is possible
about the life, the work speaks for itself and an examination of
the development of Hardress Cregan in *The Collegians* will show
the relevance of the novel to any full consideration of Griffin's
achievement and decline, particularly when it is put beside
some of the other work and considered against the background
of Daniel Griffin's often quite revealing commentary upon his
brother's complex nature.

The entry of Hardress Cregan into the action of the novel is
carefully prepared for and his character and development
meticulously presented at all points, always in deliberate
contrast with the worthy and earnest Kyrle Daly. Hardress
enters the novel when he dances with Eily at the village fête and
comes with glamorous anonymity out of the night to rescue
Eily and her father from the pestering attentions of some rowdy
youths. We catch our next glimpse of him from the window of
the Daly house. From this comfortably conventional, middle-
class dwelling the family looks out over the river and sees
Hardress skim by in his boat, the *Nora Creina*, accompanied by
the hunchback Danny Mann and a mysterious blue-coated
figure whom we know to be Eily O'Connor in flight from her
father's home. The Dalys watch as Hardress steers the boat so
close to a fishing-smack that he actually touches the stern of the
other vessel and upsets its occupants:

> A hoarse cry of 'Bear away! Hold up your hand!' was heard from
> the water, and reiterated with the addition of a few expletives, which
> those who know the energy of a boatman's dialect will understand
> without our transcribing them here. The pleasure-boat, however,
> heedless of those rough remonstrances, and apparently indisposed to
> yield any portion of her way, still held her bowsprit close to the wind,
> and sailed on, paying no more regard to the peril of the plebeian
> craft, than a French aristocrat of the *vielle cour* might be supposed to
> exhibit for that of a *sans culottes* about to be trodden down by his
> leaders in the Rue St Honoré.[18]

So Hardress sweeps by, arrogant, handsome, 'indisposed to yield', and leaves the Dalys chattering about him and his pride and his family and his gallantry. He comes to land in Chapter 12 where he is depicted as a helmsman of tremendous skill, steering his frail craft to the shore in a heavy and dangerous swell. When combating the violence of nature Hardress is completely in command.

It is only in society, as we shall see, that he becomes inadequate. As he steps ashore he tosses a revealing remark to Eily: 'A charming night this would be,' he continued, smiling on the girl – 'for beaver and feathers.'[19] The remark receives an extended explanation at the subsequent meeting between Hardress and Kyrle Daly in which these two 'collegians' outline their views on life and their sharply contrasting attitudes to society. This scene is of great importance in the book. It is inevitably a prosy affair, and Griffin's awareness of the danger he stands in of boring his reader by it is shown by the title of the chapter, 'How the Two Friends Hold a Longer Conversation Together than the Reader may Probably Approve'. The conversation is set going quite naturally. Kyrle Daly's proposal of marriage has just been rejected by Anne Chute and he can think and talk about no one else. Hardress has known her since boyhood and had fallen in love with her in his teens. He is now back from university, has met her once since his return and has found her surprisingly chilly towards him. He has reacted violently against her as a result. His comment on her is:

She is cold and distant, even to absolute frigidity, merely because she has been taught that insensibility is allied to elegance. What was habit, has become nature with her; the frost which she suffered to lie so long upon the surface, has at length penetrated to her affections, and killed every germ of mirth and love and kindness, that might have made her a treasure to her friends and an ornament to society.[20]

The subsequent discussion develops into a consideration of their respective attitudes to people and to society. It suddenly becomes clear that all is not well with the handsome and dashing Hardress. It seems he finds entry into society a difficult business but he hastens to contend that he is not, like Goldsmith's young Marlow, merely afflicted by company jitters:

My feeling is this, my dear Kyrle. New as I was to the world after leaving college, (where you know I studied pretty hard) the customs of society appeared to wear a strangeness in my sight that made me a perfect and a competent judge of their value. Their hollowness disgusted, and their insipidity provoked me. I could not join with any ease in the solemn folly of bows and becks and wreathed smiles that can be put on or off at pleasure. The motive of the simplest forms of society stared me in the face when I saw them acted before me, and if I attempted to play a part among the hypocrites myself, I supposed that every eye around me was equally clear-sighted – saw through the hollow assumption, and despised it as sincerely in me, as I had done in others.[21]

Hardress emerges as the exponent of a kind of Rousseau-istic social 'simplicity', Kyrle as the spokesman of the opposing quality, 'elegance'. The discussion is given ironic depth by our awareness that, unknown to Kyrle, Hardress has already put his precepts into practice by marrying his 'wild hedge flower', thus effectively putting himself outside the pale of the society they are discussing and setting in motion the tragic action of the novel. Kyrle Daly is made to instruct his companion in the obviosities of social usage:

'You *do* express yourself in sufficiently forcible terms when you go about it,' said Daly, smiling. 'What great hypocrisy or meanness can there be in remarking that it is a fine day, or asking after the family of an acquaintance, even though he should know that the first was merely intended to draw on a conversation, and the second to show him a mark of regard?'[22]

He warns Hardress of the dangers inherent in his attitude:

'I merely reminded you of an acknowledged fact, that when you enroll your name on the social list, you pledge yourself to endure as well as to enjoy. As long as ever you live, Hardress, take my word for it, you never will make, nor look upon a perfect world. It is such philosophy as yours that goes to the making of misanthropes.'[23]

And he concludes – ominously, in view of Hardress's secret marriage –

'It would be too late, after you had linked yourself to – to – simplicity, I shall call it, to discover that elegance was a good thing, after all.'[24]

That it is, in fact, already 'too late' is indicated a little later as Hardress settles down to sleep. He has been to see Eily secretly, in the meantime, and is irritated by her brogue and obvious lack of the social poise, for the possession of which he has only recently been castigating Anne Chute:

'Yes,' said Hardress to himself as he gathered the blankets about his shoulders, and disposed himself for sleep. 'Her form and dispositions are perfect. Would that education had been to her as kind as nature! Yet she does not want grace nor talent; – but that brogue! Well, well! the materials of refinement are within and around her, and it must be my task, and my delight, to make the brilliant shine out that is yet dark in the ore. I fear Kyrle Daly is, after all, correct in saying that I am not indifferent to those external allurements.' Here his eyelids drooped, 'The beauties of our mountain residence will make a mighty alteration in her mind, and my society will – will – gradually – beautiful – Anne Chute – Poll Naughten – independent – '25

On this Wordsworthian note he falls asleep.

He is now to embark on the curious double life he will live for the rest of the novel. He hides his wife in a cottage under the care of Poll Naughten and soon begins to spend most of his time away from her, attending a ball at his mother's house, waiting on Anne Chute, drawn to the milieu in which his mother would have him figure yet guiltily conscious of his secret marriage to Eily. His dilemma is well presented by Griffin and his gradual revulsion from his beautiful but untutored wife is skilfully charted. Witness the following effective delineation of his predicament:

He dreamed that the hour had come on which he was to introduce his bride to his rich and fashionable acquaintances, and that a large company had assembled at his mother's cottage to honour the occasion. Nothing however could exceed the bashfulness, the awkwardness, and the homeliness of speech and accent, with which the rope-maker's daughter received their compliments; and to complete the climax of his chagrin, on happening to look round upon her during dinner, he saw her in the act of peeling a potato with her fingers! This phantom haunted him for half the night. He dreamed, moreover, that, when he reasoned with her on this subject, she answered him with a degree of pert vulgarity and impatience which was in 'discordant harmony' with her shyness before strangers, and which made him angry at heart, and miserable in mind.26

In that coarse and repellent image of the potato Griffin effectively crystallises all of Hardress's growing hatred of his wife

and his increasing awareness of the appalling error into which
he has been led by putting his principle of 'simplicity' into
action. The writer is brilliantly in control of his subject here,
the imagery conveying to us with grim fidelity the exact nature
of every *frisson* of Hardress's disgust. Maddened by his situation, Hardress finally succumbs to the temptation offered him
by Danny Mann. He orders the hunchback to get rid of Eily,
warning him not to harm her but unfortunately echoing Danny
Mann's ugly image of 'the glove that fits too tight' by tossing
his glove to his servant. Danny Mann 'takes the knife to the
glove' and murders Eily, and Hardress cannot be sure, even in
his heart of hearts, that he is not fully guilty of her death.
Although he asserts violently to his mother that he did not
order Eily to be killed, he takes upon himself, in a passion of
self-accusation, the full guilt of the murder.

Padraic Colum faults the ending of the book, asserting that
the narrative is strained: 'After Danny Mann's flight from the
stable all is mechanical. The hunchback who informs on Hardress Cregan is not consistent with the retainer of the earlier part
of the story and the prisoner who sends a warning to the
bridegroom is not consistent with the informer.'[27] This is not
altogether fair to the book. Danny Mann is made to explain his
reasons for informing. Hardress has helped him to escape on
condition that he fly the country. Danny remains and encounters
Hardress on the public highway in the scene where Hardress
and Anne Chute meet the mummers and Hardress is forced
to dance with them. It is entirely acceptable that Hardress,
seeing his erstwhile servant going about in company with the
mummers instead of escaping abroad as arranged, should
become enraged and assault him furiously. Danny Mann's
resentment is equally acceptable since, in any case, an ambi-
valent attitude on the part of Danny Mann to his employer
has been prepared for from the beginning, where we are told
that the hunchback's deformed condition was brought about by
Hardress who pushed him downstairs in the course of a childish
game. That the deformed servant should veer from fidelity to
bitter resentment back to repentant fidelity is entirely acceptable, particularly in the feverishly heightened context of melodramatic guilt which the novelist builds so skilfully around his

hero. What Gerald Griffin is depicting in Hardress Cregan, then, is a young man who espouses and acts upon a naively over-simplified social philosophy, a sensitive creature incapable of compromise, a kind of Gothic George Marvin Brush.[28]

That Griffin was fascinated by this kind of character is indicated also by the only play of his which he permitted to survive when he burned his manuscripts in 1838, the tragedy *Gisippus*, in which the hero is a figure of a similar kind. The play was not staged during its writer's lifetime though a leading actress of the day, Miss Frances Kelly, expressed great interest in it, but it was produced by Macready with considerable success in 1842, Macready himself playing the leading role of the Greek, Gisippus. Gerald Griffin, in a letter written from London to his mother in America in 1824, described Gisippus as 'a fellow of exquisite sensibility almost touching on weakness; a hero in soul but plagued with an excessive nervousness of feeling, which induces him to almost anticipate unkindness, and of course drives him frantic, when he finds it great and real – at least apparently so.'[29] This could stand quite easily as an account of Hardress Cregan, and anyone who has read Daniel Griffin's sympathetic account of his brother's life will see the relevance of the description to the writer himself. That he was aware of the complexities of his own temperament is clear. His extreme sensitivity was balanced by a great natural warmth which caused him to respond eagerly to even the smallest sign of good-will from another. When, in 1827, an estrangement grew up between him and John Banim, Gerald laboured to heal the breach, and, when they were finally reconciled, wrote to his friend in the warmest terms. Throughout the correspondence, he shows himself touchingly willing to admit himself in the wrong and is clearly overjoyed when the misconceptions which caused the estrangement have been cleared up.[30]

In one of the introductory sonnets which he prefixed to *Suil Dhuv The Coiner* he writes revealingly:

> Judge not your friend by what he seemed, when Fate
> Had crossed him in his chosen – cherished aim –
> When spirit-broken – baffled – moved to hate
> The very kindness that but made his shame
> More self-induced – he rudely turned aside

In bitter – hopeless agony from all
Alike – of those who mocked or mourned his fall,
And fenced his injured heart in lonely pride,
Wayward and sullen as Suspicion's soul;
To his own mind he lived a mystery –
But now the heavens have changed – the vapours roll
Far from his heart, and in his solitude,
While the fell night-mares of his spirit flee,
He wakes to weave for thee a Tale of joy renewed.[31]

These lines indicate not merely that Griffin was conscious of the dangerous intricacies of his own nature but that he was keenly aware of the puzzling contradictions which existed between his natural warmth and his lamentable tendency to fall out with his friends and alienate them by a calculated coldness. He often displays a remarkable degree of self-knowledge, as will be obvious later from some of the verses he addressed to his friend, Lydia Fisher, but the above sonnet, while analysing his state of mind perceptively, nevertheless shows also that 'to his own mind he lived a mystery'. He emerges from his brother's biography as a Byronically handsome, warm-hearted, over-sensitive young man, badly scarred in his feelings by his encounter with the professional literary life of London, driven in upon himself, lonely, touchy, inclined to resent offers of help from friends, devoted to his Limerick home and to the local countryside where as a young man he had known his only genuinely happy hours. He was possessed of what Daniel describes as 'a notion of independence so severe as to be rarely met with'. When John Banim invited him to contribute a tale to the successful *Tales By the O'Hara Family* series, the impecunious Griffin refused to do so. Daniel, conscious of the generosity of Banim's offer, says in explanation of his brother's action: 'If there was any one object dearer to him than another in his literary career, it was the ambition of attaining rank and fame by his own unaided efforts, or at least without placing himself under obligations to those on whom he felt he had no claim.'[32]

Gerald brought to bear on his early life in London a strange kind of arrogant innocence. It is possible to trace a link between his sensitive perfectionism and his ultimate oversimplification of creative morality. The man who will not make his way through others' help, who hides away in ragged loneliness, clinging to his determination to make good by himself, is displaying the youthful unworldliness which, translated into an aesthetic attitude, becomes the distressing moral *simplesse* which was to ruin him as an artist. Fiercely ambitious of literary fame to begin with, he found the taste for fame killed by the effort of its attainment. He writes to his sister Ellen, 'I believe it is the case with almost everybody before they succeed, to wear away all relish for it in the exertion.' He wearied of the artifices of literary publicity – even Scott has to be 'puffed into notice', he says at one stage. He succeeded both as journalist and novelist – *The Collegians* earned him £800 and a considerable reputation – but either it came too late or else it all failed to live up to his rigorous, perfectionist standards. The ultimate irony is provided by his open dissatisfaction with the character of Hardress Cregan. He laments to Daniel that a wayward public will foolishly prefer Hardress to Kyrle Daly:

Look at these two characters of Kyrle Daly and Hardress Cregan . . . Kyrle Daly, full of high principle, prudent, amiable and affectionate; not wanting in spirit nor free from passion; but keeping his passions under control; thoughtful, kind-hearted and charitable; a character in every way deserving our esteem. Hardress Cregan, his mother's spoiled pet, nursed in the very lap of passion, and ruined by indulgence – not without good feelings but for ever abusing them, having a full sense of justice and honour but shrinking like a craven from their dictates; following pleasure headlong, and eventually led into crimes of the blackest dye, by the total absence of all self-control. Take Kyrle Daly's character in what way you will, it is infinitely preferable; yet I will venture to say, nine out of ten of those who read the book would prefer Hardress Cregan, just because he is a fellow of high mettle, with a dash of talent about him.[33]

This extraordinary passage, in which a writer deplores the inevitability of the success of his own artistry in the creation of a compelling character, takes us to the very heart of Griffin's mystery. '*The Collegians* was a story that used to write itself', he was to tell his brother Daniel, and the remark is more significant than at first appears. The book surely 'wrote itself' because its central character was, in some devious way, some kind of expression of the writer's own creative dilemma. It was a dilemma he was to fail to solve. He was never again to find writing come easily. 'I have got such a cobbling feeling about literature since I began to make my regular winter bargains,' he writes to a nephew. He wrote *Tracy's Ambition*, a book much less flawed than *The Collegians*, but a lesser book. It is a highly competent continuation of the social analysis which forms the background of the earlier novel. In it Griffin achieves a masterly exposé of the social abuses of rackrenting landlords and the miseries of an exploited tenantry but it is a dark grim book without the compelling brilliance of *The Collegians*. It lacks a Hardress Cregan, a hero whom Griffin can invest with the characteristics which come to vivid life along his own pulses. Tracy's self-sufficient ambition can set a train of grim events in action well enough but it cannot, as Hardress Cregan's arrogant inadequacy does, fire a book into a blaze of melodrama.

In *The Collegians* Griffin found the perfect story for his intense and tragically narrow gift of characterisation. The book is the inevitable climax of his achievement. Hardress Cregan is certainly melodramatic. He oversimplifies life, plunges into a disastrous situation, lunges this way and that in his efforts to escape, sins dreadfully, repents passionately – it is all extremes.

But it was a similar 'simplicity' which caused his creator so much daily difficulty in his own life and brought him eventually to destroy his manuscripts and abandon at once the world and his craft. Hardress refuses to make the compromise with society which Kyrle urges on him. He will carry his Rousseau-istic *simplesse* into his practice in life – and does so, with disastrous effects. This creature of extremes, starting from a hatred of sham, transgresses his social code, reacts violently to the resultant predicament and brings ruin upon himself. It is a fictional analogue of Griffin's own predicament. Hardress's social morality is as simple, as unsophisticated as Griffin's artistic morality. They are both sensitive, warm-hearted, full of 'nature', passionate and intense. They both have an over-simplified view of life and they both murder what they love: Hardress murders Eily; Griffin tries to destroy his work. Surely Griffin's penetration of the ambiguities of the character of Hardress is made possible because of some war within himself between two sharply opposed views of life and art, views which might be described in Kyrle Daly's words as 'simplicity' and 'elegance'. Hardress is brought to ruin by acting on his 'simplicity', but when he finds that it is just as possible to love the well-born and haughty Anne Chute and be loved by her in return it is too late to profit by his new sophistication and he is reduced to a frantic impotence. His stasis parallels his creator's.

The Collegians is Griffin's greatest work because it combines a hero whose psychology paralleled the author's own with a vivid depiction of a society in decay. It is the combination of personal with social which makes this novel memorable. Hardress's predicament is made poignant though the book is not always well plotted. He is a possible person, a character whom the author understands, at least in part, and whose setting he knows very well indeed. Thrown over all this is the romantic gloom of mountains, woods and streams and the result is a memorable melodrama which at times verges on being a great psychological study. Griffin was to write other novels but never again did he achieve the kind of Macbethian, doom-laden atmosphere of his best-known work. Hardress is an amateur of life, just as Griffin is essentially an amateur of letters. The Hardress who expresses his impatience of social *politesse* is the Griffin who feels that he is wasting time on story-telling while others are doing real work like doctoring or teaching and who therefore tries to qualify himself in the law, thinks of becoming a priest, teaches young local children their catechism and finally retires from the world. *The Collegians* is not merely Gerald Griffin's masterpiece. It is also the master key to an understanding of his development and decline.

5

Regional writer, historian, moralist, lover

In 1829 Griffin published, in addition to *The Collegians*, another three-volume work containing two stories of about equal length, *The Rivals* and *Tracy's Ambition*. Both make clear his growing interest in and profound compassion for the wretched state of the Irish peasantry. In spite of the intrusive melodrama of *The Rivals*, both that story and its companion piece give a memorably realistic picture of the grim world inhabited by the Irish peasant of the first quarter of the nineteenth century.

The Rivals (1829)

The melodramatic story concerns a Methodist beauty named Esther Wilderming, loved by two suitors, Francis Riordan and Richard Lacy. The former is a romantic young rebel who gets into trouble when he interferes with the police work of the more conservative and calculating Lacy. Riordan has to flee the country and take refuge in South America but, before he goes, he binds Esther to be true to him forever. When his death is reported, she yields to family pressure and becomes engaged to Lacy. She dies of grief and Riordan returns from abroad to find that she has just been laid to rest in the family vault. He removes her from the tomb, she miraculously revives and they are married. Lacy does his fiendish worst but fails to prevail against his rival or his love for Esther. He dies repentant. Told like that it sounds the most arrant melodramatic rubbish. This absurd plot, however, is merely the necessary, novelistic façade for a really effective piece of rustic realism which is sometimes very funny and often disturbing. Griffin sets his story in County Wicklow, around the beautiful vale of Glendalough, and seizes

the opportunity to describe the small and lively rustic world of
the place. In the depiction of Mr Lenigan's hedge school he
achieves some of his most celebrated comic effects.[1] So vividly
is the schoolhouse brought to life that we find ourselves bitterly
regretting that Griffin did not pursue this vein of his abilities
and eschew the melodramatic effects in which he so often
indulges. The lesson in 'consthering' Virgil's *Aeneid*, conducted
by Mr Lenigan's Classical assistant, is both hilariously comic in
itself and richly relevant to the entire history of verbal acro-
batics in the Anglo-Irish novel. The teacher leads his rustic
scholars vigorously through a passage from the *Aeneid*, contriv-
ing on the way a marvellous, forced marriage between the
sonorous splendours of the Latin and the hilarious vividness of
the Anglo-Irish idiom of the south of Ireland. Here, clearly, is
beginning one notable strand of Anglo-Irish literature, the
flamboyant, thrasonical, vigorous line which is to include
Carleton, Lever, Boucicault, Joyce, Flann O'Brien and Brendan
Behan. Griffin's polymaths are the harbingers of such complex
achievements as the 'Oxen of the Sun' episode in *Ulysses*.

The world of *The Rivals*, however, though productive of such
hilarities as these, is essentially a grim place. The author's tone
is a combination of the sombre and the sardonic:

About this time one of those provincial insurrections broke out,
which were usual during the last few centuries, amongst the discontented peasantry. Arms were taken, contributions levied for
ammunition, floggings and cardings inflicted on the part of the
insurgents; while the usual preventives were adopted by the local
government. The district was proclaimed, and some hundreds of
people were transported, but, strange to say, they still continued
discontented.[2]

The precise nature of the cause espoused by Riordan is never
very clearly indicated. He is said to be the author of a clever
escape plan which rescues some prisoners from Lacy's police
custodians when they are on their way to deportation but, in
the court-room scene at the climax of the novel, he denies that
he has been a rebel against the crown: 'You have laid treason at
my door, and I will point it out lurking behind your own. You
have called me rebel, falsely called me so, but I will make the
same charge good against yourself, by evidence as palpable as

matter.'[3] Thomas Flanagan equates Riordan with Robert
Emmet but, in fact, he hardly emerges in so clear a light.[4] His
rebellious doings are on a local rather than a national level and
he experiences no difficulty in taking his place in society at the
novel's end. As often with Griffin, however, the highly-flavoured
histrionics of the principal actors are based on a clearly observed
foundation of reality. The miseries of the Irish poor are made
constantly clear. In an early scene we are introduced to the
home of Mr Kirwan Damer, Esther's uncle and guardian, a strict
Methodist with a tendency to proselytise his Catholic depend-
ants. His brother-in-law, Tom Leonard, instructs him in the
facts of Irish life and the paradoxes which he has ignored:

'Ah, now, come, Damer, keep your cant for the preachers, and talk
like a man. It is very easy for you and me to sit down by our coal
fires, and groan over the sins and ignorance of the poor, starving,
shivering cottagers, while we drink our champaign and hermitage;
but, heaven forgive us, I'm afraid that we'll fare otherwise in the
other world, for all our hypocrisy, while these poor devils will be
reading the Bible in paradise.'
'Fie, fie, Leonard, you grow more profane.'
'Do you know what John Wesley said?'
'Any thing that escaped the lips of that saint must be comfortable.'
'Very well. He said it was impossible for a Christian to expect to
ride in a coach on earth, and go to heaven afterwards. Pick comfort
out of that if you can.'[5]

The turbulence of Irish life is reflected in lively discussions in
shebeens and at death-beds. Mr Lenigan's brother, Davy, is
made the spokesman of the sort of liberal conservatism which
was probably Griffin's own political faith. In the scene at the
inn, in the village of Roundwood, he delivers a lengthy harangue
on the subject of the Vestry Bill Act and the Sub-letting Act
which have been the company's principal topics of conversation
and, in the course of his speech, manages to glance at Catholic
disabilities generally:

We surmounted the times, gentlemen, when the priest was hunted
with more diligence than the ravenous wolf, an' as for the schoolmasther – (there was some tittering amongst the girls) – an' as for
the schoolmasther, he was searched for as a vigorous sportsman, on
the banks of the Nore, would search for his game . . . The time is now
past when the poor bewildered Catholic, in his state of starvation,
would not be allowed to keep a horse worth more than five pounds,

and when he would not be allowed to keep one foot of the land of his forefathers under a lase, an' even spakin' the language of his country was a crime.[6]

He concludes his harangue by warning his listeners that violence will only play into the hands of their enemies:

the surest and most expeditious way to break all those chains, is to live paceable with those savages that daily want to raise us to rebellion, to observe the laws in the sthrictest manner, to avoid night-walkin' as the root of all our misfortunes, and, of all the world, to beware of any secret societies, for I can assure you, with truth, that all who belong to any such community are of little consequence in any concerns, inless in violating the laws, an' going headlong to the gallows.[7]

In a sense, therefore, Griffin manages to have his 'rebelly' cake and eat it. He effectively brings home to his readers the genuineness of the peasants' grievances while constantly managing to suggest that all would be well if the laws were decently administered. Corrupt local politicians are the villains of the piece and are, essentially, as much the enemies of all loyal, middle-class citizens as of the peasants whom they more obviously oppress. The novel constantly affords us revealing glimpses of the troubled tangle of the life of the Irish poor, living close to the breadline and subject to savage penalties for transgressions which their appalling conditions render inevitable.

Tracy's Ambition (1829)

This second story is in every way more successful than *The Rivals*, more powerfully imagined, more forcefully and succinctly realised. It is the first-person narration of one Abel Tracy who is ruined by falling into the grip of obsessive ambition. The work has an almost Jonsonian force, with Abel possessing the comprehensive significance of a 'humour'. In his rendering of the main character Griffin displays considerable sardonic insight into Abel's psychology and employs it to involve us both with Abel himself and the turbulent times in which he lives. Abel is in every way an in-between character. He is, first of all, neither gentleman nor peasant but uneasily placed between two social levels and at the mercy of both:

I was one of a race who may be considered the only tenants of land in my native Island. Our castle owners, above us, and our cabin holders, below, are both men of estate; while we occupy the generous position of honorary agents to the former, serving to collect their rents in a troublesome country; and of scapegoats on whom the latter are enabled to repose the burthen of rent, tythes, and county charges.[8]

The admirable brevity of this compares favourably with the much more leisurely and flaccid style of the corresponding description of that other 'middleman', Mr Daly, in Chapter 4 of *The Collegians*. Abel, himself a Protestant, compounds his median status by marrying a well-to-do Catholic, Mary Regan, whom he rescues romantically when her horse bolts. Griffin drives through these necessary preliminaries with unaccustomed speed and skill and in his short opening chapter manages to introduce Abel, marry him to Mary Regan and sketch effectively the well-bred scorn with which her brother, Ulick Regan, greets the match. Abel is to continue to smart at his elegant brother-in-law's contempt throughout the story. Ulick chides his sister for marrying secretly without his consent and promptly departs from Ireland, while Abel and his bride settle down at Cush-lanebeg in reasonable comfort and set about rearing a family. Mary plays the part of intermediary for the local peasantry in any suit they make to her husband and for a long time he heeds her advice and, as a consequence, is highly regarded by the people.

His difficulties begin with the arrival in the area of a magistrate named Dalton whose express business it is to sniff out disaffection and generally play the part of government spy. He holds out to Tracy the promise of preferment, playing on Tracy's desire to climb the shaky ladder of a turbulent and disordered society:

A magistrate himself, and toiling hard for preferment, he had expressed a wish for my co-operation, and opened to my view prospects of personal advantage which I found it difficult to regard with that indifference of which I boasted. The influence which a little exertion, such as he recommended, would procure me among the people of the neighbourhood; the emoluments, trifling indeed in appearance, but yet capable of being improved into a return worthy of consideration; the rank to which it would lift me among the gentry of the country; the post which perhaps it would become my right to occupy among the representatives of ancient families, at sessions and

3 Richmond House, the home of James and Lydia Fisher

4 The North Richmond Street Monastery in 1838

5 'The Wake' (cf. *The Collegians*, Chapters 33, 34)

6 'The Hedge School' (cf. *The Rivals*, Chapter 7)

assizes; no insolent bailiff nor Peeler to slap the court-house doors in
my face; no impertinent crier to pick me out of a crowd with his long
white wand, and bid me 'Lave that, an' make room for the gentlemen
o' the Bar – ' I figured to myself all these flattering circumstances,
while I passed up and down our flagged hall, under such an agitation
of spirits as I had seldom before experienced.[9]

Dalton's adored son, Henry, falls into debt and the besotted
father calls on Abel Tracy for help. To retain Dalton's favour
Tracy hands over his daughter's dowry of six hundred pounds
and from then on is at Dalton's mercy since the money is not
repaid at the time agreed and Tracy's domestic affairs begin to
disintegrate. Dalton continues to dangle before him the promise
of preferment, and Tracy, conscious of his folly but driven on
by his fatal flaw, soon passes from comfort and happiness to
wretchedness and destitution. Dalton is engaged in persecuting
the local people in the name of law and order and is prepared
to go to any lengths to obtain convictions, planting evidence,
suborning informers, bribing and threatening. Once he allows
himself to be identified with Dalton, Tracy earns the hatred of
the local people who had previously trusted and depended upon
him. He falls victim to the terrorism which is inevitably bred
of the vile social conditions and the cynicism of Dalton's
administration. His wife, Mary, is killed by a band of masked
attackers and he himself gravely wounded. He loses everything
he has treasured until he is left with no object in life except the
unmasking of Dalton. The hero's emotional turbulence is well
charted by Griffin. At various points in the narrative Tracy
perceives and even analyses accurately his own decline but
always makes the necessary compromise with evil which forces
him yet another step along the road to moral disintegration:

Yes, I thought, I will first withdraw myself from his power, and
secure a compensation for my losses, and then I will denounce and
cast him off. Until then, until I am secure from the effects of his
resentment, beware, my temper, how you suffer your vulgar prej-
udices to appear!
I listened, meanwhile to a long dissertation of Dalton's, on the
state of the Island, on the weakness of my nature, on the gain to be
acquired by activity and *firmness*, and other stimulating subjects.
But his pains were superfluous, for I had already determined to
sacrifice my consciousness of right, and enter into a compromise with
treachery.[10]

An effective part of the novel's moral structure is that Tracy's machinations are made finally to founder in total absurdity. Ulick Regan returns from exile to take a hand in his niece's fortunes. Tracy fails to recognise him, changed as he is by long residence in a tropical climate, and in any case fails utterly to comprehend Ulick's plans for his niece, Tracy's daughter, Eileen. Tracy absurdly jumps to the conclusion that Ulick wishes Eileen to marry a ridiculous drunken bachelor named Purtill and, labouring under this complete misapprehension, Tracy introduces this gaby into his house as Eileen's accepted suitor. He persuades his daughter to dismiss her fiancé, Rowan Clancy, who is, unknown to Tracy, the suitor favoured by Ulick. Tracy needlessly distresses his daughter, throws his house into an uproar with the silly doings of the egregious Purtill and is made to look wonderfully foolish when his mistaken assumptions are exposed. Ulick's long-standing contempt for his brother-in-law seems justified by this climax and indeed by Tracy's weakness of character throughout the novel but, in spite of this, Griffin succeeds in retaining our regard for his all too vulnerable narrator. He is always more victim than villain and it is impossible to dislike altogether a character who is so often depicted at a disadvantage in his own account of his adventures. His enemy, Dalton, is brought low by the same forces which murdered Tracy's wife. Young Henry Dalton is brutally murdered by a peasant whom Dalton has repeatedly wronged and the broken-hearted father never recovers from his terrible loss. Tracy's ambition and the net of intrigue and calculation in which it involves him are ultimately exposed as the trivial irrelevancies they really are, and Abel Tracy himself complacently reveals at the very end how little he has learnt after all:

For myself, I now lead a peaceful life among a circle of merry friends. My ambition is entirely set at rest, and I think if I could only succeed in obtaining the commission of the peace, which I am at present using every exertion to procure. I should be a contented man for the remainder of my days.[11]

It is appropriate that Griffin should have woven one of his most successful stories around the idea of an obsessive ambition. Intensely ambitious himself at the outset of his career, he gradually lost his taste for worldly success and found his work as a writer becoming increasingly distasteful to him. More and more he came to feel that his pursuits as an author were somehow irrelevant to the real concerns of a busy world in which he found himself sharing a house with two hard-working doctors, his brothers William and Daniel. For the depiction of Abel Tracy he reached within himself and applied profound convictions and insights concerning excessive human aspirations to his keen perception of the social ills of his day. In his effectiveness as a narrator, Abel Tracy recalls Maria Edgeworth's Thady Quirke in *Castle Rackrent*. Dangerously balanced between two classes, two religions, he inhabits a moral no-man's-land which Griffin charts with instinctive skill. This short and powerful work is altogether lacking in the longueurs which affect the much better-known novel, *The Collegians*. *Tracy's Ambition* possesses an impressive moral coherence and offers convincing glimpses of small-town life and the day-to-day existence of the country people. Griffin's Ireland often appears as a pullulating pit of restless helots but the depiction of their miseries is made all the more convincing by the fact that the novel is far from unrelievedly sombre. Indeed, there is a generous measure of the sort of comedy which would be at home in the 'R.M.' stories of Somerville and Ross when Griffin recounts the hilarious doings of the corps of yeomanry of which Abel Tracy is a member. His eye for comic detail is nicely evidenced in the second lieutenant who brushes his eyebrows against the grain to give himself an appearance of military ferocity. At the same time, the comedy is effectively used to suggest the chaotic state of the forces of law and order.

The malign attitude of authority to the Irish poor is voiced with memorable viciousness by Dalton:

I think them a base, fawning, servile, treacherous, smooth-tongued and black-hearted race of men; bloody in their inclinations, debauched and sensual in their pleasures, beasts in their cunning, and beasts in their appetite. They are a disgusting horde, from first to last. I enquire not into causes and effects; I weigh not the common cant of misrule and ignorance; I look not into historical influences; I speak of the men as I find them, and act by them as such . . . I hate the people.[12]

The savage bitterness of the oppressed is voiced by the old hag,
Mrs Shanahan, whose son has been shot dead by Tracy during
a midnight attack by insurgents:

You did this for me, Abel Tracy, an' the prayer I was goin' to offer,
'till you hindered me, was that the Almighty might do as much for
you. If I had the arms or the sthrength of a man, I would'nt be talkin'
to you this way. But though I'm weak, I have strong friends, an'
they have you marked. You can't sthrike a bush in the country from
this day, but a friend of Shanahan will start from it against you. Ah,
Abel Tracy, there is no law for the poor in Ireland, but what they
make themselves, and by that law my child will have blood for blood
before the year is out.[13]

Maria Edgeworth had seen the peasantry through the eyes of
Thady Quirke as that dangerous serf had gazed out through the
cracked panes of Castle Rackrent. Griffin, through his narrator
Abel Tracy, brings the people Thady saw to vivid life for us,
and in this short but powerful novel we stumble with them along
the muddy roads of a barbarous and bitter land, we feel them
huddling their wretched rags about them, we inhabit with them
their miserable cabins and feel their winter cold. Many of
Griffin's personal tensions must have been generated by the
clash between his powerfully realistic vision of the Irish world
about him and the demands of his comfortable, middle-class
background. A different sort of man would have either joined
in the exploitation or perhaps undertaken an active campaign
against it. Griffin, intelligent, sensitive, peace-loving, separated
by birth and fortune from the mass of his countrymen but
utterly unable to identify with their oppressors, worked out
the logic of the situation and came to his own conclusion, that
the only hope for his country and its people lay in improving
their lot by educating them. He would have agreed with Davis's
cry, 'Educate that you may be free', and we can see in the tragic
vision he displays in *Tracy's Ambition* the reason for his eventual
decision to join a teaching Order dedicated to the educational
betterment of the Irish poor.

His lengthy concluding note to the work makes clear his
attitudes and his didactic purpose. He first distinguishes between his own work in fiction and that of the Banim brothers,
John and Michael, in their well-known *Tales by the O'Hara
Family*:

They were the first who painted the Irish peasant sternly from the life; they placed him before the world in all his ragged energy and cloudy loftiness of spirit, they painted him as he is, goaded by the sense of national and personal wrong, and venting his long pent up agony in the savage cruelty of his actions, in the powerful idiomatic eloquence of his language, in the wild truth and unregulated generosity of his sentiments, in the scalding vehemence of his reproaches, and the shrewd and biting satire of his jests.[14]

His own intention, he says, has been to depict a gentler Ireland:

We have endeavoured in most instances, where pictures of Irish cottage life have been introduced, to furnish a softening corollary to the more exciting moral chronicles of our predecessors, to bring forward the sorrows and the affections more frequently than the violent and fearful passions of the people.[15]

He then goes on to convey his views on the course of Irish history and on the character of the Irish people as it has revealed itself through the ages. The Irish character, he states, has been astonishingly consistent in its fidelity to its native leaders, its devotion to the Church, its hatred of the conqueror. The credulity of the Irish has been matched only by the fury of their resentment when that credulity has been betrayed:

It might be an interesting investigation to examine into the origin of those varieties in character which appear to be so hereditary, and which can only be broken up by a difference of political situation, and by a more extended system of education. But at present we only wish to speak of the character and condition of the Irish peasant as he is.[16]

When he goes on to consider what steps should be taken to improve the lot of the Irish peasant, Griffin is in no doubt as to what needs to be done:

Poverty in nations, as in individuals, is the parent of licentiousness, and man must cease to feel the pangs of hunger before he can find leisure to embrace goodness. Will England, then, remain insensible to the personal afflictions, to the continued agonies of this long-suffering and long-neglected class of men? Will she permit their natural protectors, untaxed, to squander their resources abroad, and to return at long intervals only to increase the oppressions of the people?[17]

The immediate need, clearly, is for an improvement in the political position of the Irish peasant and for a radical revision of attitude by the holders of the land. Only then will Ireland cease to be a drain on the British Treasury and a source of English ignominy before the nations of the world.

In both *The Rivals* and *Tracy's Ambition*, Griffin writes with a powerful realism which is undimmed by the occasional melodrama of the plots. Both stories provide the reader with an unusual insight into the daily harshness of the lives of the Irish poor. Country roads with their travelling people, small towns with their poor markets and their beggars and prostitutes, paupers' cabins and paupers' graves, informers, 'nightwalkers', all pass before us in a sombre panorama of national desperation. Griffin has come a long way from the youthful detachment of his London days.

The Christian Physiologist (1830)

In Chapter 12 of the *Life*, Daniel describes the growth of Gerald's religious scruples in regard to his work. More and more, he became convinced that he was wasting his time and that it was impossible for the writer of fiction to control the creative passion and direct its power to proper, moral ends. Daniel reports him as saying: 'I see you, and William, and every one around me constantly engaged in some useful occupation, and here am I spending my whole life in the composition of these trashy tales and novels, that do no good either to myself or anybody else.'[18] It is clear from the account in the *Life* that Daniel struggled hard to combat his brother's moral and aesthetic scruples but it is equally clear that his arguments fell on deaf ears. As the situation worsened, Gerald began to impose upon himself a Dedalus-like regimen of regularity, the very strictness of which is symptomatic of his increasing distaste for the literary vocation:

He became more systematic than ever in the disposal of his time; punctual as the striking of the clock in his hours of rising and retiring to rest; and, singular to say, though his interest in his literary labours had nearly lost all its freshness and force, he went through them each day with a most exact and scrupulous industry, looking on them as his only occupation, and therefore feeling that, as a matter of duty, they ought to be done well.[19]

It was at this time that he began work on *The Christian Physiologist*, an overtly didactic work with a specific moral aim which is clearly programmed in the Preface to the book: 'We have sought, by adding to that knowledge of his moral nature which his religious education supplies to the young Christian, such a knowledge of his physiological existence, of the wonders of his own frame, as might assist him in the observance of his heavenly duties.'[20] That Griffin himself was far from confident that the public would take kindly to his fictional moralisings is indicated by his account of the curtailment of the original project for a much more elaborate work:

It was intended at first to arrange in a popular form, and illustrate by amusing fables, the whole science of physiology; but it soon appeared that such a design must necessarily extend to a greater length, and demand a greater sacrifice of time, than would be warranted by the uncertainty of its reception with the public. We have therefore confined the undertaking at present, to the five external senses; which, if the public approbation should not warrant the completion of our design, will form a little work, complete in itself.[21]

In a lengthy footnote to the Preface, Griffin adverts to the erroneous views he had held at an earlier stage of his life and expresses profound regret for the mistaken opinions of his youth and for the bad example he may have set some of his young friends.

The Christian Physiologist contains, in addition to the five tales 'illustrative of the five senses', a long chapter entitled *Of the Intellect* and a concluding tale, *A Story of Psyche*, which is 'intended to represent the human Soul, or Will'. The second story in the book, *The Day of Trial*, illustrative of the sense of Hearing, had earlier appeared, under the title *The Deaf Filea*, in *The Juvenile Keepsake* in 1829. The first two stories in the volume are prefaced by an account of the functioning of the organs in question (the eye and the ear) and Griffin seems to have drawn freely on his brother's medical text-books in this connection, as Daniel indicates in his biography:

The portions of this work which related to the structure and functions of the organs of sense, showed such an intimate knowledge of anatomy and physiology, that many persons imagined they could not have been written without the assistance of some medical man, and therefore that Dr Griffin or I must have had some hand in them; but this was so far from being the case, that though we could not help wondering what it was that made him every day pull down our medical books, and give himself so deeply to the study of anatomy, neither of us had the slightest conception what he was at until the work was completed.[22]

Each of the five tales is also prefaced by a chapter on the use and government of the sense under review.

The stories themselves are generally unimpressive. *The Kelp Gatherer* is a moral tale about a patient widow who endures blindness until, as a reward for her submission to God's will, she is cured of a cataract by a surgeon and is thus enabled to see her son, his wife and children for the first time since their return from America. It is noticeable that, although the story is set in Ireland, Griffin does not here equip his characters with a regional idiom. They are made to speak a correct, indeed formal English. *The Day of Trial*, the only story not specifically prepared for this volume, is rather more elaborately constructed and more effective. Madaghan, chief poet to the arch-king of Erin, has one son who is both deaf and dumb. Unknown to the despairing father, the son's disabilities are miraculously cured and he sets about training as a minstrel in secret. He enters for the contest which is to decide his father's successor as chief poet and, having won, reveals his secret to his delighted parent. Some of the ornate detail of this story resembles that of the long historical novel, *The Invasion*, which was soon to follow and for which Griffin had been collecting material for some time.

The Voluptuary Cured is, as its title suggests, an account of the reform of a nobleman bored by worldly pleasures. On the advice of his physician, he abandons the frivolous gaieties of the London season and sets out for his estates in Ireland. He puts up at a dreadful hotel in Waterford where his pocket-book is stolen and from which he eventually sets out, penniless, to travel to his agent's residence. He arrives in time to save a peasant from eviction and then discovers that his physician and the inn-keeper have been benevolently in league against him for his own good. The 'theft' of his money has been a hoax and Lord Ulla, in returning to his responsibilities as landlord, discovers the pleasures of a simple life and the satisfaction of

doing one's duty. Mild fun is poked throughout at the Englishman's notion of Ireland as a wild country full of brigands and
thieves. Lord Ulla, like Maria Edgeworth's Lord Glenthorne, has
his eyes opened to his duties and to his own best interests.
Despite its heavily moralistic tone, this is one of the more
effective stories in the book and, in Lord Ulla's distaste for
London and in the mild satire at the expense of English ignorance of Irish life, one occasionally catches a glimpse of Griffin's
own sensations and attitudes. *The Self-Consumed* is a short and
improbable tale illustrative of the evils of self-indulgence and
luxury. Its detail is, once again, similar to that of *The Invasion*,
with considerable emphasis on items of antique ornament,
weapons and dress. This type of description is even more lavishly
employed in *The Selfish Crotaire*, the story illustrative of the
sense of Taste. This is set in the same era as *The Invasion*, the
period of the Viking invasions of Ireland, and is clearly indebted
to the lengthy researches Griffin was making in preparation for
his historical novel, details of which were included in his
Common-Place Book A, which is described and discussed at a
later stage of this chapter.

The Christian Physiologist concludes with a chapter on the
Intellect and the long, fanciful allegory of the progress of the
Soul, *A Story of Psyche*. The account of the intellect is interestingly premonitory of Griffin's eventual flight from the world,
and *A Story of Psyche* is really an extension into the theological
and moral fields of the old argument carried on between
Hardress Cregan and Kyrle Daly about the conflicting claims of
'elegance and simplicity'. Psyche, or the Soul, thrust out of
Paradise, is torn between the conflicting claims of Imagination
(Hardress Cregan) and Judgement (Kyrle Daly). Imagination
bedazzles Psyche into ignoring the sober warnings of Judgement, and, when Psyche has sickened of the delights of the
senses and begun to fear the consequences of the evil she has
perpetrated in the world through surrender to sensual delights,
Imagination proves her greatest foe, filling her mind with horrid
images of punishment and terror. Psyche is beset by images of
the torments of Hell and, in desperation, turns to Philosophy
for help but Philosophy is lost in the mists of scientific enquiry
and can offer no true help to the questing spirit. Finally, the

Almighty takes pity on Psyche and guides the searching Soul to the path of righteousness. Judgement is discovered at the foot of the Cross, and Psyche takes up the Cross and lives a life of self-denial and patient virtue. This, Griffin's brief version of a pilgrim's progress, is in no way theologically startling but the whole piece is interestingly analogous to Griffin's own life and very revealing of the type of thinking which lay behind some of his major decisions. At times the language employed anticipates passages from his later correspondence. Psyche, at the end, is thus depicted: 'Psyche has often been heard to say, that her life is happier than when abandoned to the dominion of her own servants, she trod the fertile valleys of the world, inhaling its sweetest perfumes, and banquetting upon its richest fruits.'[23] Years later, Griffin was to write to a friend in very similar vein, after he had himself retired from the world and was working as a teacher in the Christian Brothers' house at Cork: 'it seems curious even to myself, that I feel a great deal happier in the practice of this daily routine than I did while I was roving about your great city, absorbed in the modest project of rivalling Shakespeare, and throwing Scott into the shade'.[24]

Thus, *The Christian Physiologist*, even if of no great literary merit in itself, suggests something of the flavour of his next novel, throws considerable light on the kind of thinking which had shaped Griffin's past development and, further, forecasts his eventual retirement from the world.

Common-Place Book A: The Invasion (1832)

At the Christian Brothers' house at North Richmond Street, Dublin, where Griffin was received as a novice in 1838, there is preserved a most interesting common-place book of the author. Since Griffin attempted to destroy the bulk of his papers before retiring from the world, anything which survived the holocaust acquires thereby a kind of Sibylline interest merely by virtue of its survival. *Common-Place Book A*, however, is of absorbing interest in itself and in relation to the novel of which it is the basis, as it will be the purpose of the rest of this section to demonstrate. It is written in a copy of Taylor's printed form of common-place book, rebound in black half-leather with black grained paper boards, and has a printed paper label on the front board inscribed *Common-Place Book A*. It measures nine inches by seven and contains 330 pages, with a two-leaf insertion and coloured map at the beginning and a single-leaf insertion between pp. 292 and 293. The entries are written in dark ink and remain clear and easy to read. One short pencilled entry on p. 3 has faded somewhat. There are remarkably few corrections or erasures. The volume is equipped with an alphabetical Index of two letters on a leaf and had a set of eight labels, A to H. The labels B to D are missing which suggests, tantalisingly, that there may have been three other such books which are now lost. On the *verso* of the marbled end-paper there are the following inscriptions:

Common-Place Book of Gerald Griffin presented to St Mary's Library by the Very Revd B. T. Russell, Prov.O.S.D.
Presented by the Prior and Community of St Mary's to the Christian Brothers, North Monastery, Easter, 1921.

Enquiries to the Prior of St Mary's, Cork and the Rev. Br. Superior of the North Monastery, Cork have failed to uncover any other such volumes.

In *Common-Place Book A* the novelist recorded the mass of material which he collected for his historical novel, *The Invasion*, published in 1832. Daniel relates how Gerald embarked on preparations for this historical novel soon after the publication of *The Collegians* in 1829:

Gerald had no sooner completed *The Collegians* than he began to turn his attention to the study of ancient Irish history, believing that there were many peculiarities in the usages of early times which would admit of being blended with a story, and would keep up that interest in the public mind, about the decline of which he was always apprehensive. He was deeply taken with this study, and says, in a letter to his brother, 'I am full of my next tale – quite enthusiastic – in love with my subject, and up to my ears in antiquities at the London Institution.'[25]

In March 1829 his researches took him to Dublin. He wrote to his brother William:

I have done a great deal here at the Dublin Library, which is a tolerable collection, and I am promised an introduction to the Dublin Institution – also rather extensive. I do not wish to leave Dublin

until I have smelted all the antiquarian lore in those two mines,
which, by the way, is much more abundant than I expected. I have
already learned to think enough for my first purpose, but as in architecture 'a little stronger than strong enough' is the great maxim, so
a little more learned than learned enough is a grand requisite for a
historical work.[26]

So determined was he to prepare himself properly for his historical novel that he deferred publication of it until 1832. With
characteristic integrity he was determined that his novel should
be based on genuine and painstaking research. It is interesting
to speculate why Griffin, at the moment of his greatest success
with the publication of his best-known novel, *The Collegians*,
should have turned aside to such antiquarian pursuits as absorbed him from 1829 until the publication of *The Invasion* in
1832. There is a clue, perhaps, in a letter which he wrote from
Pallaskenry to a friend in London in February 1828 in the course
of which he has the following to say about Irish history:

There is a history which the world wants – a history which would do
service to a people, and confer immortality on a historian (if properly
executed). If I had even a moderate degree of talent – and with this
talent the opportunity, the industry, (*that* I should command,
however, I think,) the wisdom requisite for a good historian, I would
undertake it in preference to any work whatsoever – I mean, as you
may conjecture, a history of Ireland . . . Are there not men who would
feel a *pleasure* in painting the convulsions of a powerful people,
labouring under a nightmare for ten centuries?[27]

It should be remembered that, when he wrote this letter, a
year after his return to his own country, Griffin was still painfully
close to the experiences of his London period, those three fateful
years of struggle and bitter disappointment during which he
lost for ever the first, fine, careless rapture of his early ambition
and began to win for himself what he was to describe as the
'half of a name'. He had struggled in the alien capital to have
his plays accepted and in this he had failed utterly. He had
finally succeeded in making a living by working for the literary
journals of the day, by parliamentary reporting, by all sorts of
hack-work. His literary dreams had faded very fast and he had
felt himself an outsider in a city he hated. It is possible to see
his antiquarian studies and his determination to write an
historical novel as a logical and integral part of his development.

His deep consciousness (expressed in the letter of February 1828 quoted above) of the gloomy, disastrous nature of Ireland's history for the ten centuries preceding his own gives us our point of departure. *The Invasion*, set in the halcyon days *before* the invader ravaged Ireland is, in a sense, a grandiose piece of patriotic nostalgia on the part of this talented and rootless man in desperate search for an identity, personal, national and artistic. Thomas Flanagan has noted how, during his time in London, Griffin made friends principally with foreigners, other expatriates.[28] He never put down roots in England and his early difficulties and disappointments obviously gave him a particular horror of London.

Yet, as a writer, he knew that London was the place where he must make his mark. He is sometimes, in certain moods, strongly attracted to the society of his literary peers. An excited letter from Dublin to his brother William on April 11, 1829 says that he 'will take the world as it comes from henceforth, and crush ceremony to pieces. I long to meet Lady Morgan and to know Miss Edgeworth.'[29] His considerable success with *The Collegians* gave him the entrée to literary society. Scott praised him.[30] Maria Edgeworth wrote in a letter to a friend about '*The Collegians*, in which there is much genius and strong drawing of human nature'.[31] Griffin clearly felt the attraction of the cultivated literary world of his day. His own letter of April 11, 1829 contains this revealing passage:

It would, after all, be a great advantage that people of rank and influence should know and be interested about one, and it is worth something to know what fashionable society is. They are the people whom one writes to please, and it is well to know what pleases amongst them.

This is my sober, business-like reason for wishing to know them; but take the honest truth – the pleasure is more than half the motive. This, after all, is really the only rank in which I could ever feel *at home* – in which I could fling off the *mauvaise honte* – talk – laugh – and be happy. But once again – that pang! I must work hard and get the antidote.

Why was I not born to a fortune?[32]

That is one of Griffin's voices, the voice with which he speaks when, for a brief space, success, professional and social, raises him to a pitch of delight and social confidence which he seldom attains. The other voice follows immediately, in the same letter:

> If you were, says a little voice, you would never have known the Irish peasantry – you would never have written *The Collegians* – nobody would know, nobody would care a fig for you.
> Thank heaven that I was born poor – but, oh! heaven, do not keep me so![33]

That last jocose prayer holds the secret of his restlessness. It is that which sends him back to the early history of his country to depict a period when Ireland was not a drab, misgoverned, English colony but a centre of learning and culture to which the people of the larger island sent their children to be schooled. Griffin had, after all, proved with *The Collegians* that he could cut a figure in the larger literary world of his time. He had had a great success but he was finding it increasingly difficult to treat his peasant countrymen merely as fodder for the regional novel. His drift is increasingly towards a genuine sympathy for his fellow-countrymen's miseries. *The Invasion* is a search for his origins and a search for solace. He had written, in a Joycean phrase, of 'a powerful people, labouring under a nightmare for ten centuries'. For Griffin as for his more celebrated successor in the Irish novel history was a nightmare from which he was trying, in his own way, to awake.

Common-Place Book A and the novel based upon it form a remarkable record of his flight from an intolerable present into a richly romanticised past. It provides references to over sixty works on history and mythology, ranging from *The Book of Lecan* to Bede's *Martyrology*, from Alfred's *Translation of Orosius* to Holinshed's *Chronicles*. The book records detailed information on a wide range of topics connected with the ancient Irish and the Danes. The novel was to be set in the eighth century and the writer records masses of detail about the dress, weapons, architecture, fighting habits and character of the Danes and the Irish of that period. An old map of Ireland showing the country divided into Leath Mogha (in the south) and Leath Cuin (in the north) is inserted at the beginning and occasional reference is made to this map throughout. Interspersed here and there are brief suggestions about the plot of the novel, for example on p. 30:

Chap. 1: The Vikingirs described. State of Northern Europe. Character of the Sea Kings. Descent of Thorgils and their subjugation of Ireland. Devastation of Armagh. Thorgils and Malachy become kings, under what circumstances. View of state of country etc.

This entry was clearly made at an early stage of his planning of the novel because, in the finished work, this sketch of the opening chapter is not adhered to and the novel, instead, opens quietly in Ireland, with the actual invasion and the account of the Vikings held over until considerably later in the book.

Although later editions of *The Invasion* (published by Duffy of Dublin) were to carry an apologetic note about Griffin's amateur status as an antiquarian, and Professor Eugene O'Curry was to be called in to contribute explanatory notes of a more academically respectable kind, nevertheless Griffin's preparatory reading was of an impressive nature and its range and extent explained the huge quantity of detailed information contained in *Common-Place Book A* and eventually fed into the novel itself. The origins and history of the Vikings are sketched, with an account of their character, their battle practices, their religion, their funeral customs. There is a great deal of information on the history of ancient Ireland and the development of Irish Christianity, with accounts of the dress, living conditions and practices of the early Irish, their schools and bardic courts. Considerable attention is paid to the Druids whom St Patrick displaced and much of this detail finds its way into the novel eventually (for example, the story of Patrick's shocking the Druids by lighting his huge fire before theirs on the eve of Samhain). The notes lay considerable emphasis on the splendour of ancient Ireland and on the advanced state of its learning. Frequent reference is made to gold and gold ornaments being in common use among the rulers, and their patronage of poets and historians is stressed. The Irish contribution to learning and Christianity is frequently mentioned, a typical entry being as follows:

When Charlemagne founded the universities of Pavia and Paris, in the eighth century, Claude Clement and John Scot, both Irishmen, were appointed directors and first introduced the Birede, Biretrum, or doctor's cap, and the gold ring or the insignia by which they preceded all ranks but the nobility. (p. 228)

The notes soon become a roughly chronological survey of early Irish history, from pre-Christian times to the period after the Danish invasions and the record seems to conclude on the book's final page (p. 300) as the last entries, which record the survival of the Danes in the trading towns, have a note of finality about them. There follow twenty-one pages of a carefully kept Index (two letters on a leaf) with entries from A to W.

The most obvious interest which attaches to *Common-Place Book A* is that it is the evident source-book for one of Griffin's later novels and the great mass of detailed information which the writer compiled was to give *The Invasion* an authenticity which is, in places, a great advantage to it but which is often a dead weight, particularly at the beginning of the novel where the writer grossly overindulges himself in antiquarian description at every possible opportunity. This aspect of the novel was glanced at tartly by a contemporary reviewer in the *Literary Gazette* for Saturday, January 7, 1832 who commented: 'An epic, a novel, a treatise on political economy, and an antiquarian essay, are materials that do not assimilate. We will first allow our author to speak for himself, and then say why we think his efforts will not be rewarded with popularity.'[34] The novel itself is rather better than the reviewer suggests. Admittedly it begins very tediously and one soon wearies of the writer's determination to load every rift with the results of his antiquarian researches. Once the story gets under way, however, there is a certain interest in the confident depiction of a remote period and Griffin's reading would seem to have had this beneficial result, that it enabled him to move naturally enough through the remote times he is describing. It is, of course, a sentimentalised Ireland, full of richly apparelled chieftains and exotic Druids. There is little mention of the common people who, if they appear at all, do so merely as extras in the crowd scenes of a very glamorous production. The novel is leisurely in the extreme and perhaps the most curious aspect of it is that the invasion from which it derives its title barely happens. In this connection the entry on p. 30 of *Common-Place Book A* about the burning of Armagh (quoted earlier) is most revealing. In the book itself this incident never takes place. It was evidently abandoned by the novelist but would seem to indicate that he had, at one time, intended to write about the Vikings' devastation of the main centres of Irish Christian civilisation. In the novel as he eventually wrote it the Vikings make a landing (in Munster), but this action is subsidiary to the quarrel between the hero, Elim, and his uncle, Baseg, and the invaders are repulsed pretty rapidly in the closing chapters.

What seems to have happened is that the focus of Griffin's interest changed as he wrote the book and turned from antiquarianism into channels already familiar to us from his previous novels. The book's strongest focus is on the character of Elim's Saxon friend, Kenric, who is yet another in the gallery of proud, discontented solitaries already so familiar to us in the work of this novelist. Kenric is a Saxon who is sent by his parents to be schooled in the sister island and he meets Elim at school and forms the friendship which is at the centre of the book. In terms of *The Collegians*, Elim is the Kyrle Daly, Kenric the Hardress Cregan of this novel. Kenric is always proud, solitary, inflexible in his opinions. He travels in Europe and achieves a superficial scholarly fame with a slight treatise on astronomy. The turning-point of his career occurs when he enrages the local Saxon ruler, Duke Elfwin, by contradicting him stubbornly in a trivial debate about the dating of Easter, thus losing the duke's favour and having to set out on his travels which eventually lead him into a guilty involvement with the Norsemen, the enemies of his Irish friends. He melodramatically saves Eithne, Elim's betrothed whom Kenric also loves, from death at the hands of the Vikings and dies at his home after a melodramatic illness bordering on madness. Pride is his besetting sin and the passages in which he deplores this failing have a familiar ring for the reader of Griffin's novels. He is from the beginning an outsider. At school, only Elim's kindness saves him from himself and, once their ways divide, Kenric is doomed by his own proud, inflexible nature to live and die unhappily. Griffin's preoccupation with this sort of character is, perhaps, nowhere more startlingly displayed than in this book where the treatment of Kenric's character is allowed to take precedence even over the carefully amassed historical detail. In the last analysis this is, in spite of all early appearances, a novel about Kenric rather than an historical novel.

Judging from *Common-Place Book A*, it would seem to have been the novelist's intention to write a vigorous account of battles long ago. In the event, though the Vikings, their beliefs and practices are elaborately described, they barely touch the shores of Ireland and we get instead a novel about a tormented Saxon solitary. This change of direction on the writer's part also renders irrelevant his early insistence on the dangers of faction among the Irish chieftains (a theme which Griffin probably wished to relate to the factious politics of the Ireland of his own day). If the book had shown an Ireland ravaged by the Vikings from without and torn by dissensions from within, the point about the dangers of faction would have been forcefully demonstrated. Since, however, Elim successfully repels the brief Viking attack at the end, much of the earlier detail about differences among the Irish chieftains seems ultimately irrelevant and the novelist seems to be aware of this when he closes his story by glancing briefly into the future and refers to the larger and more successful Viking invasions which lie ahead. In the light of the revealing entry on p. 30 of *Common-Place Book A*, it would seem reasonable to suggest that Griffin set out to write an historical novel about an Ireland already occupied by Viking invaders but that he finally wrote instead yet another elaborate exploration of the proud solitary who is always, in the region of character, his most obsessive interest.

There is one section of *Common-Place Book A* which has no connection with *The Invasion* but is of peculiar interest to the biographer as it sheds much light on the way Griffin's ideas were developing at this time (about 1830). Between pp. 113 and 143 he breaks off his exploration of ancient times to note his views on two important works which he was then reading. These are Locke's *On Human Understanding* and Rousseau's *Emile*. On pp. 118 and 119 there is also a short section headed 'Edgeworth on Education'. It is fortunate that, on p. 118, Griffin inserted a note to indicate that he finished reading Locke's work on May 1, 1830. This is the only date in the book and helps to place it for us. Pages 113 to 118 are occupied with a discussion of Locke's views on religious differences as expressed in his treatise on *The Conduct of the Understanding*. This involves Griffin in a careful discrimination between 'faith' and 'belief'.

He distinguishes between them by contending that, while belief can be erroneous, faith cannot, a point which evidently matters to him as he returns to it briefly much later on in a note on p. 287 where he states that belief 'implied trust, and there can be no trust where is a mathematical certainty . . . Certainty is not belief, it is knowledge.' Locke distinguishes between the religious zealot and the person who is prepared to survey all religions with 'an equitable and fair indifference', and Griffin rejects the notion of 'an equitable and fair indifference' as sophistical. If you have the true faith, he says, why play meaningless games by pretending that you haven't? Without enquiring too nicely into the theological intricacies, what importantly emerges for the student of Griffin, at this point, is the inflexible certitude of his views.

For all the sweetness and gentleness of his nature, this is a mind like a rat-trap. Once the spring has snapped on a truth it will not again release it for further examination. He expresses himself in mathematical images of certainty:

A faithful Catholic for instance is bound to believe as firmly in the truth of his creed as that *four* is the double of *two*, although the grounds of his conviction are different, the former belief being dependent on the will, the latter not. Now the less time a man expends in listening to the opinions of those who assert that two and two make five, the more time he will save for better purposes. (p. 114)

and again:

if I hear a man gravely contending against the self-evident fact that the three sides of a rectangular triangle are equal and if I, for impatience, will not hear him this does not mean that I have a bias the other way, but merely that I have a bad temper. (p. 118)

The gulf between Griffin's purposeful certainty and Locke's equally purposeful uncertainty is profound. We begin to understand Griffin's often puzzling critical intolerance as displayed in such unfortunate jingles as the one about the Romantic poets:

Wordsworth, and Coleridge, and Landor, and Southey,
Are stupid, and prosy, and frothy, and mouthy.[35]

In fact, in the course of his discussion of Locke, he employs the adjective 'romantic' in a clearly pejorative sense:

The idea that mankind could be taught to judge aright, when passion urges them to judge wrong, in cases where the matter is left to their own understanding appears to me no less romantic than Lord

Shaftesbury's fancy of practising virtue for its own sake and not for
the love of its Author or the influence of hope and fear. (pp. 116–17)

These are, once again, the arrogantly convinced tones of Hardress
Cregan arguing for 'simplicity' as against 'elegance' and they
show how close artistic disaster looms. Empathy of an authorial
kind is going to be more and more difficult for this writer. Fresh
light is thrown on the important passages in Chapter 12 of the
Life in which Daniel describes Gerald's decline into an aesthetic
paralysis and his own efforts to argue his brother into a more
reasonable frame of mind with common-sense arguments which
stood no chance against the novelist's compulsive idealism:

I mentioned to him also what I was informed a certain clergyman, a
man of genius and information, and highly esteemed in his diocese,
had said on the subject: 'That he conceived it one of the greatest
misfortunes to society, that, by a sort of general consent, an engine
like the drama, capable of influencing so many millions to good or
evil, should be left in the hands of the vicious and corrupt. That, as
it has existed, and will exist to the end of time in all civilised countries, the common sense and benevolence of the thing was to make it
as available to the purposes of virtue as it is now to vice. As to its
being at best imperfect, and not without danger to some, that was the
fate of all human exertions at good. Our instruments are always
imperfect, let our aims or objects be what they may . . . One can
effect no good without the possibility of some evil, for which, when
one does his utmost to avoid it, he cannot be responsible.' Gerald,
though he would not admit the applicability of such reasoning,
replied to it so slightly as showed what little interest he took in the
subject, often dismissing the argument with some little pleasantry
and a smile, which made it clear that the time when it could have
affected him was gone by.[36]

It is clear that Griffin was no longer susceptible to suggestions
that the writer is a necessarily imperfect instrument in an
imperfect universe. His intellect also rejected Locke's idea of
'an equitable and fair indifference' on matters of belief and,
more and more, Griffin was to find it impossible to assume the
attitude of artistic 'indifference' to the behaviour of his fictional
creatures. The human sympathy and devouring curiosity about
man and the universe which are life to the novelist were going
down before a clutch of intransigent religious and moral convictions. Immediately after the section on Locke comes a brief
passage in which Griffin takes the Edgeworth system of education

to task for proposing 'a too great worldliness' as its object. The
following extract, recalling Griffin's youthful ambitions and
their rapid decline, has a strongly personal tinge:

This love of worldly distinction, of exaltation, so contrary to the
Christian precept, is the cause of the ruin of many promising characters. I grant that it is a passion hard to be subdued in youth, particularly when it comes under the veil of a love of independence, but
if we cannot subdue it, for heaven's sake let it not be fostered. (pp.
118–19)

Between pp. 120 and 143 Griffin discusses Rousseau's *Emile*.
He professes not to share Rousseau's horror of boarding-
schools, claiming that families must eventually be broken up
and that 'it is good that the nestling should be accustomed to
short flights at first since it is doomed eventually to be banished
from the home of its infancy'. There are some overtones here,
surely, of Griffin's response to his own youthful separation from
his parents and the bulk of his family at the time of their emigration to America. He evidently finds Rousseau, at least in some
ways, a more congenial philosopher than Locke, as he writes
about him in a more relaxed and friendly fashion:

Where Rousseau is in the right no man is more delightful. He is easy
– elegant – witty – profound – But where he merely speculates –
merely theorizes – where in fact he is in the wrong it is easy to see it
for he at once gets angry and scolds people. Compare for instance his
irresistible denunciation of swaddling clothes and hired nurses with
his phillipic against public schools. (p. 121)

There follows immediately after this a passage which is so
revealing of Griffin's peculiar, solitary nature that it deserves to
be quoted in full:

Rousseau's notion of a perfect confidence between master and pupil
is I fear chimerical. This perfect confidence could not be accomplished
even if they were as he wishes they should be of the same age. There
is only one state of perfect confidence on earth – it is that which
exists between a Catholic penitent and his confessor. Here alone there
is no reserve – here alone the heart is truly laid bare – and the soul
exposed in its true colours. The confidence of the most intimate
friendship must still have some reserve and it is right and necessary
that it should. Even if a man were guiltless of any crime, the very
suggestions of nature herself, and the temptations to which the
purest minds are liable render it necessary there should be a degree of
secrecy. (p. 121)

Here speaks the touchy, sensitive, lonely man who suffered so wretchedly in London and, towards the end of his life, sent so coldly dismissive a message to his beloved Lydia Fisher in the waiting room at North Richmond Street.[37]

There follow some twenty or more pages in which Griffin considers various parts of the *Emile* and faults many of the great Romantic's theories. There are sizeable quotations in the original French, which would seem to indicate that Griffin had acquired at least a competent reading knowledge of that language. He is sometimes quite penetrating in his comments. On facile philanthropy he writes:

I cannot but think that there is more of self-love than of philanthropy in the mere spinning of theories. It is easier and more pleasing to indulge the imagination than to serve the public. It is one thing to do good and another to dream of it – one thing to be useful and another to be eloquent. (p. 122)

And, on the natural treatment of disease:

It is lost time to talk of applying natural remedies in an unnatural state of society. To say 'let nature be the physician' is in a word to say 'let all the world be reformed' a very easy thing to say and delightful to contemplate, but saying it and thinking it will cure nobody. (p.122)

His strong dislike of many of Rousseau's notions about children lends unusual force to his comments:

Vicious human nature – depraved nature – he knew well – but he has not even a conception of the good and healthy human heart, such as it is when filled with the love of God and regulated by principles of virtue. He is to the human mind what Dr Baillie was to the human body – its morbid anatomist. Of the sound subject he knows nothing. (p. 124)

Throughout, his remarks are based on a rejection of Rousseau's concept of the State of Nature and on his own belief in the doctrine of Original Sin. Sometimes an unexpected but very Irish gaiety breaks through:

'Ayez donc soins de le promener souvent, de le transporter d'une place à l'autre, de lui faire sentir le changement de lieu, à fin de l'apprendre à juger des distances.' Imagine a nurse hawking a child to and fro and telling you when you ask her what she is about, that she is *taichin' him distance, the crathur!* (p. 129)

His own formidable standards of rectitude are frequently
revealed, as on p. 132: 'The agony which the remembrance of
crime occasions is not always penitence. Remorse may sin on,
repentance never will. The vengeance of God and of nature is
not the merit of the criminal, it is his punishment.' There is a
curious passage on p. 134 in which he traces the growth of
piety, unexpectedly maintaining that manhood is less inimical
to piety than childhood. Often his comments on both Locke
and Rousseau reveal a keen intelligence which revels in argument and which can express itself with considerable force and
some wit. Here and there, though, can also be seen glimpses of
those aspects of his character which were to prove so stultifying
to irs- ... whe**'s absolute conviction of the essentially
sol** ... formidable, almost
imp** ... l rectitude which
sad** ... m, prevented him
fror ... produced in him a
disa**, ... th
C** ... ment of the most
abso**, ... of Griffin and it is
inde** ... so much else has
peris** ... on for the writing
of *The Invasion* it is a monument to his impressive professional
conscientiousness and is of evident importance in relation to the
novel for which it is the source-book. It also makes clear a
revealing historical nostalgia on Griffin's part. It is evidence of a
certain kind of patriotic escapism, a flight from the harsh
realities of an intolerable Irish present to the halcyon days of a
glorious past. Finally, the thirty pages of comment on Locke
and Rousseau between pp. 113 and 143 bring us close to the
writer's mind and thought in a most revealing manner. It is,
perhaps, too much to hope that *Common-Place Books B, C and
D* will now be found but it is fortunate that this one at least
survives, to bring us into contact with a considerable talent
whose early decline is one of the great tragedies of early nineteenth-century Irish fiction. This phase of Griffin's career, from
the publication of *The Collegians* to 1832, shows evidence of a
changing attitude to his native country and a deepening sympathy for the terrible plight of the Irish poor. It also reveals in

him an increasingly moralistic bent, allied with a growing tendency to indulge in a revealing kind of escapist historical nostalgia.

GERALD GRIFFIN AND LYDIA FISHER

The year 1829, which saw the publication of his most enduring fiction, was to prove memorable for Griffin for other reasons also. It was in this year that he formed the warmest personal association which was ever to come his way outside his immediate family circle. It was a characteristically cruel irony that the woman who aroused his ardour was of a different religious persuasion and, in any case, already happily married. She was Lydia Fisher, wife of James Fisher and daughter of a well-known writer, Mary Leadbeater (1758–1826), author of *Cottage Dialogues Among the Irish Peasantry* (1814) and *The Annals of Ballitore from 1768–1824*. The Fishers were Quakers and lived near Limerick. At the time of their first meeting Lydia Fisher was about thirty, some three years older than Griffin himself. She too had done some writing, though she did not achieve her mother's fame.

It was Griffin's journalistic pieces which first brought him to the notice of the Fishers. They read and admired some of the Irish sketches which he had written for the London journals but, as has already been noticed, these were all published either anonymously or under pseudonyms so that it was some time before the Fishers knew the name of the writer whose work they had been admiring. They then came to know him through his more serious publications, first of all *Holland-Tide*, then *Tales of the Munster Festivals* and particularly through *The Collegians*. After the publication of his best-known novel Gerald was invited to visit the Fisher home and 'having spent an evening there, he returned to Pallaskenry, delighted beyond expression with his new acquaintances'.[38] It is clear from such letters as survive that at this point Gerald fell in love not just with Lydia but with the entire Fisher family and he did so because he found them 'a literary oasis in what I thought a desert of utter and irreclaimable dullness'.[38] Recently returned as he was from London and Dublin, elated with the success of his most ambitious work so far, he was delighted beyond measure to find close to his Irish home a highly congenial family who shared his intellectual and literary interests, who admired his writings and welcomed him warmly into their happy family circle.

The letters which survive from this period bubble over with boyish pleasure in his new-found friends. In mid-summer, after a trip to the Lakes of Killarney with them, he wrote warmly enthusiastic letters to both James and Lydia. James had been the organiser of their trip and had coped with the costs of accommodation, boats, guides and so on and had evidently proved most efficient at the task. Gerald affectionately charges him with excessive generosity since Gerald's share of the expenses works out at a mere two pounds and ten shillings:

You are the prince – the emperor of fellow-travellers. Two pounds ten shillings for a fortnight at the Irish lakes – for ascending mountains – diving into vallies – for ponies, guides, boats, dinners, breakfasts, beds, servants, Kenmare, Bantry, Glengariff, echoes and all! J—, you are an immortal man. What would you think of accompanying me over the Simplon? I had made a calculation last winter in London, when I thought of visiting the Eternal City, and found that I could go by Paris, Lyons, Turin, Florence, etc., and return for something about forty pounds. But do you come with me, I will put my purse in your hands, and I hope to get off under five or six. In the mean time, my dear fellow, look over your Killarney accounts again, and oblige me, for I am sure you have made a mistake greatly in my favour.[39]

The companion letter to Lydia indicates that she has met Gerald's sister, Lucy, and found her 'graceful'. Gerald urges Lydia to visit the Griffin home so that he may 'dovetail your hearts together'. He encloses a copy of Lesage's *Le Diable Boiteux*, which he warmly recommends to her but goes on to say that he will give Butler's *Hudibras* to James so that the latter can read it to her as he thinks fit, for it is 'a queer sort of a funny book'. The letter grows more warmly affectionate as it goes on and Gerald is clearly most eager that the acquaintance should grow and prosper:

L—, write me longer letters when you write again, and don't write about coming or going anywhere, but put the whole of L—'s mind and a piece of L—'s heart upon the paper, and it will be to me as welcome as the summer; and don't talk about forgetting, for if that begin on

either side it will be on yours. To me such a friendship as I promise
myself yours will be, is a rare blessing, such as a poor author wants
to console him for a great deal of chagrin and disappointment; to
keep his heart sweet amid its struggles with an ugly world.[40]

Lydia's letters to Gerald have not survived and in attempting
to analyse the precise nature of the relationship between them
we are, therefore, largely dependent on the selection of Gerald's
letters which Daniel supplies in Chapters 11 to 13 of the *Life*.
These are not always complete and are often undated though
it is often possible to deduce the approximate dates fairly
accurately from internal evidence. Further light is cast on the
relationship by some of the letters of Gerald which survive in
the possession of the Christian Brothers. Apart from the letters
the only further clues are supplied by the verses which Gerald
addressed to Lydia from time to time. Daniel quotes a number
of these in his biography and we can form a fairly accurate
judgement on the nature of Gerald's feelings for Lydia Fisher
and of the progress of his attachment by reading the letters and
verses together. When we do this what emerges is an emotional
graph strangely analogous to the curve of Griffin's literary
career. That is to say that the affair begins ardently, then sours
for a while before finally mellowing into a more pedestrian form,
until it is finally stamped out by the scrupulously perfectionist
Griffin who climaxes the affair by refusing to see Lydia when
she calls on him at his Dublin monastery. In a similar mood, he
climaxed his literary career by burning his manuscripts. This
wilful self-abnegation is his only final solution to all his dilem-
mas.

In the beginning, however, all goes well. He is soon writing
to Lydia again to tell her of an accident which has befallen
himself and Lucy while out driving in a gig. Lucy has sustained
a dislocated elbow and Lydia has evidently promised to visit
her. It would also appear that some poem written by Lydia has
contained a flattering reference to Gerald, or so he chooses to
believe at any rate:

Thank a certain sweet poetess in your neighbourhood for the allusion
contained in a certain sweet poem, if my vanity has not misapplied
the meaning of the stanza. Ah, you are dear people all of you – a
literary oasis in what I thought a desert of utter and irreclaimable

dullness! So much for my native city. For yourself, dear friend, what shall I say? That delicious as are your assurances of sympathy you are indeed right in supposing that to me they are utterly unnecessary. I could not meet you with the same pleasure, nor leave you with the same regret, if it were otherwise.[41]

He is at this time working on *The Christian Physiologist* and asks for her comment on some of the stories: 'I send you, in the hope that it may afford you some entertainment, a *fresh* manuscript – the concluding story of my volume on the Senses. As you liked the style of the deaf Filea you may like this also.'[42]

Then the mood changes and we hear once again the ominously touchy voice of the Gerald who found it so fatally easy to quarrel with his friends. His irritation this time has been caused by Lydia's expressing doubts about the sincerity of some verses he has addressed to her. He writes her an angry letter, then repents of his anger and thinks better of sending her the letter and writes instead to explain how his fury has passed away and wiser counsels prevailed. In a characteristic flurry of roundabout self-accusation and explanation he poses to Lydia a question which, in view of subsequent events, is not without irony:

when I think of the delightful summer which has just flown by; when I think of Adare, of Killarney, of Glengariff, of Tralee, of Tarbert, of Askeaton, of Richmond, and of the happiness which I felt in the growth of our friendship amid those scenes, I often ask myself: Is it possible the time should ever arrive when a friendship like ours – warm – noble – elevated – as I often thought it, should fade away in cold suspicion and unworthy negligence? On my part I answer, never; on yours – why – a – never – I believe also; but then to talk of you having 'the appearance of my friendship!'[43]

At this time he is about to leave for London to see his publishers and sends Lydia 'a string of rhymes on that story of Cathleen' and pays her elaborate compliments:

I am too great a sinner ever to have wished for a window over my heart, as Nebuchadnezzar, or King Pepin, or one of those great philosophers said formerly, and yet (must you not think this strange?) I could agree to have a pane or two inserted in that little edifice in which you are lodged, for there you are, unchanging and immovable, somewhere, I think, about the left auricle, in which they say the blood flows calmest and purest.[44]

From London towards the end of 1829 he wrote to Lydia a
long letter in which he supplied details of his daily regimen
which included along with his literary labours daily sessions
with the dumb-bells for 'I intend to become a prodigy of mus-
cular strength.' His tone is a mixture of gaiety, sentiment and
fraternal raillery. He even finds time to tantalise his inamorata
with talk of his own need for a wife:

All I should require now to make this mode of life perfectly agreeable
is a fair companion, and I think I have a chance of getting one to my
taste. She is a decent woman, not above forty, rather cleanly than
otherwise, and not squinting very much, and at any rate, if she should
not please me, there is a Jew's meeting in the city, at which T— and
I sometimes attend on Saturday nights – I, of course, as you will
suppose, in the hope of 'bettering myself,' and T—, as he would have
a person believe, with the view of hearing a theological discussion;
but don't suppose I mean to insinuate anything to the contrary.[45]

Just before Christmas of the same year he writes again at length
to sympathise with Lydia on the death of her sister. In the
course of his elaborate condolences he assigns himself his chosen
role as Lydia's brother, a description which appears repeatedly
in his letters to her:

Be assured that you have found a brother who will always be ready
with his sympathy in whatever way you may require it; who is
proud of his sister and devoted to her wishes; and whose pride and
happiness it will be to supply, by a pure and earnest devotion of
spirit, the void which may be left in her affections by the severing of
earlier and dearer ties, though this should be even in the least
degree.[46]

His contact with the Fishers has now lasted little more than
six months, but that his puritanical scrupulosity is already
coming to the fore is obvious from a letter to his sister, Lucy,
at the beginning of 1830. This was written exactly one month
after the previous letter in which he had assured Lydia of his
fraternal concern for her. The letter to Lucy is not included in
the *Life*. It is one of those which has survived in the possession
of the Christian Brothers. In it Gerald first assures Lucy
that he intends to do penance for earlier pleasures by spending
'a Lent as black as the pots'. He continues, in a revealing post-
script:

I had a letter from Lydia Fisher on Friday in which she speaks most affectionately of you – give her my affectionate love and tell her that I will write to her as soon as possible. Ah Lucy – Lucy don't tell her though that I fear – with all my admiration of – affection for her I fear we have devoted too much time to one another for our other duties. Don't for your life, you rogue you, say a word of this to her or anybody else.[47]

It has taken only half a year for him to change from loving ardour to pious caution. Yet, far from severing the connection with the Fishers, he actually went on holiday with Lydia and her children in the autumn of 1830 to the sea-side resort of Miltown Malbay. He appears to have appointed himself a sort of unofficial uncle to the Fisher children of whom he writes with obvious affection. They were often permitted by their parents to stay with the Griffins at Pallaskenry and Gerald became for a time tutor to the eldest Fisher child, Josey. After a time the difference in religion brought this arrangement to an end, to Gerald's great regret. Shortly afterwards he made the little boy a toy boat and wrote tenderly to his father, James Fisher, asking him to allow Josey to come to Pallaskenry to sail the boat on the lake there.

James Fisher was the recipient of a very different sort of letter shortly after this, when Gerald wrote to him in the unpleasingly formal and unbending tone which he sometimes adopted to even his dearest friends. It would appear that Gerald may have begun to put into effect the feelings of moral caution he had voiced to Lucy and had been seeing rather less of the Fishers than of yore. James seems to have remonstrated with him about this and drew from Gerald a pompously sententious rebuke:

The last part of your letter gave me pain, for you have entirely mis-apprehended what I wrote. Be assured, my dear friend, that I did not intend you should infer that because I hoped to see you often when you were alone I should not be glad to see your family also, or that my friendship for them was less than for yourself. I am aware that both to you and Lydia my conduct for some time past has appeared wrong, and, perhaps, ungrateful. Although I do not think it my duty to speak freely with you (without your express desire) of the principles on which I have acted, yet the intimacy which subsisted between us last year, and the sincere friendship which I retain for you and for every member of your family, render it, I believe, necessary

that I should offer some explanation. Above all, you will not consider what I say obtrusive, when you remember that it was your
own misapprehension that drew it from me. It is true that my time
is not, nor cannot be, allotted as formerly, but it is equally true, that,
whatever may appear, there is no loss of friendship nor of gratitude
on my part towards you all, and that nothing in this world would give
me greater happiness than the having it in my power to spend as
much time in your society as formerly; but I felt, strongly felt, that I
could not do so consistently with my other obligations; and have I
not before told you, that they and you are not the only friends from
whom I felt myself obliged to withdraw a large portion of my time?
Did I not tell you that I visited at Richmond oftener than amongst
my near relations? I do not wonder you should think me cold; but
believe me, that you deeply err in thinking so. I know well that I
must appear so; but I know well also that it was my duty to act as I
have done; and I hope the time may come when you will see this as
plainly as it appears to my own mind.[48]

By the same post he writes Lydia an extraordinarily prudish
and moralising letter in which he faults both Milton and Byron
and begs her to use her influence in her circle of friends to
condemn 'any book which tends to inflame what is already but
too ready to take fire'.

It is clear that the Fishers must often have had to exercise
considerable patience to endure the shifts of mood undergone
by their volatile literary friend in Pallaskenry. Because of missing dates on the letters in the *Life* it is not always easy to chart
the precise fluctuations in the relationship but it seems clear
that, in general, friendly relations were maintained in spite of
Gerald's occasional petulance and censoriousness. To be fair
to him, this side of his character appears only rarely in the
letters to Lydia and most of the time his letters bubble with
affection and are full of lively chit-chat about all sorts of things,
from politics to literature, from his affection for the young
Fishers to his brotherly feeling for their mama. At one point he
sends her, in return for a gift of hers, a cup made out of a
coconut, carved and bound in silver and charges her to find some
use for it on every first of May. After Josey's departure he
whiles away the time by drawing and painting and sends Lydia
the pictures on condition that he be asked to Richmond to hang
them.

One letter which survives among the papers in the possession

of the Christian Brothers is unusually tantalising. It is from
Gerald to his sister, Lucy, and appears, from internal evidence
to belong to the year 1831. So devious is the phrasing that one
can now only speculate as to the writer's exact meaning, but it
is certainly within the bounds of possibility that the circumstances alluded to so circuitously in the letter may have arisen
out of his relationship with Lydia. The letter is addressed from
Limerick to Miss Griffin at Miltown Malbay and, after some
preliminary banter about a hat and sunshade which he has sent
her, and some items of family news, Gerald continues:

And now dear Lucy to answer your letter – for all this is foreign to
the principal matter on which I had to write. Do not imagine that I
ever accused you of want of candour to me – even in those cases where
I longed that you should speak and where I was tempted to be discontented at your silence – I have – and always had an unbounded
reliance on you for that virtue in which I fear I am naturally as well
as habitually deficient – a holy and clearsighted prudence – and
whatever you said or said not, did or did not, that went against my
wishes I attributed to that and was I think, satisfied. But, my dear –
dear Lucy – I have something more to say which may prevent your
blaming yourself in the least. The want of candour was I fear my
own, for I frequently thought of saying to you 'Lucy I do not of late
ask you any questions, because I suppose if there was anything you
think I ought to know you would tell me of it.' Had I said that as
perhaps I ought to have done all difficulty would have removed to
you at any rate – but I was inconsiderate enough (without reflecting
how hard it was for you to act where you had so little to guide you)
to suppose that you would do so without my desiring it. God – our
good merciful God has however ordered these things at least for our
happiness – oh, may he grant that it be also for our real advantage!
My heart is greatly, greatly lightened – may He enable me to remember this year and to keep that heart steady and grateful in his service.
Great – great indeed is my happiness in the restoration of the deepest
friendship I had ever formed – for who that has not experienced it
can tell the bitterness of loving with a true, a fervent, and external
love – and yet of being accused of coldness, of neglect, or of a culpable
fanaticism, more Pharasaical than Christian. Ah my dear Lucy –
thank God I was not wholly acting on my own counsel as you truly
judged, and if I did permit caution to extend itself to excess – if I
did give pain without real necessity, I think I can say – can hope
that my motives and my intentions were not wholly selfish. But of
all this my dear Lucy will say there has now been quite enough and I
sincerely hope that it will be the last time that either romance or
'nonsense' will ever give any disquietude to the minds of others or

to my own. 'Nonsense' is sometimes charming – and charming too
at first sight – but it required a trial to know how much more delicious
is duty.[49]

'The dearest friendship I had ever formed' may refer to Lydia.
Equally, of course, it may refer to his intense affection for Lucy
herself. Or perhaps Lucy may have taken it upon herself to
tackle Gerald about his coldness to the Fishers, that deliberate
withdrawal from their company which produced the chilly letter
to James, noticed earlier.

At any rate, Gerald, as always, settles for duty in the end in
preference to what he chooses to call 'nonsense', and 'romance'
is also given its *congé*. In the years that followed he remained
friendly with Lydia and wrote to her often. He kept her informed of his travels in England and in Ireland, wrote to con-
gratulate her on the birth of another child at the end of 1831.
In March of 1833 he sends her a long, detailed and lively
account of the visit he paid with his brother, Daniel, to Thomas
Moore at Sloperton Cottage the previous November. References
to Lydia which appear in Gerald's letters to other members of
his own family are always affectionate and brotherly rather than
ardently amorous. Some of his letters seem to imply that Lydia
regularly expressed admiration for his writings and tried to
encourage him in every way possible, but he disclaims the
praises she offers him and tells her on one occasion that poor
health has prevented him from attaining real greatness. That
she was keenly aware of his defensive and vulnerable temperament is clear:

And now, why does dear Lydia talk of reluctance to send her free
thoughts to her affectionate friend, and doubt of the spirit in which
her letter might be received? How could Lydia doubt of the spirit in
which such affectionate and generous counsel would be taken? How
could it be taken, except with gratitude, to the writer, and happiness
in the thought of possessing a friend so kind and so interested?[50]

As late as the middle of 1835 he is writing affectionately and
sending her some verses written years before during the holiday
they shared at Miltown Malbay, verses full of tender suggestive-
ness and sentiment:

> Because my heart is lightly shaken,
> By haunts of early joy forsaken;

Because the sigh that Nature heaves
For all that Nature loved and leaves,
Now to my ripening soul appears
All sweetly weak, like childhood's tears.
Is friendship, too, like fancy, vain?
Can I not feel my sister's pain?
Ay, it is past! where first we met,
Where Hope reviving thirsted yet,
Long draughts of blameless joy to drain,
We never now may meet again.[51]

Daniel Griffin, usually so cautious about what he includes in
the *Life*, gives us some remarkably revealing verses which
indicate clearly that Gerald had certainly confronted the full
implications of his feelings for Lydia Fisher:

Hues of darker fate assuming,
Faster change life's summer skies;
In the future, dimly glooming,
Forms of deadly promise rise.
See a loved home forsaken,
Sundered ties and tears for thee;
And, by thoughts of terror shaken,
See an altered soul in me.

Never in those tended bowers –
Never by that reedy stream –
Lull'd on beds of tinted flowers,
Young Romance again shall dream.
Now his rainbow pinions shaking,
Oh! he hates the lonesome shore,
Where a funeral voice awakening,
Bids us rest to joy no more!

Yet, all pleasing rise the measure
Memory soon shall hymn to thee,
Dull for me no coming pleasure,
Lose no joy for thought of me.
Oh, I would not leave thee weeping,
But, when falls our parting day,
See thee hush'd, on roses sleeping,
Sigh unheard, and steal away.[52]

He must have realised very clearly that only 'forms of deadly
promise' could emerge from any attempt on his part to indulge
his feelings for her. It was a particularly cruel stroke of fate that
caused him to fall in love with a married Quaker, a dutiful wife

and mother. Daniel concludes the *Life* with some verses which provide Gerald's own very precise definition of the relationship along with an acute perception of his own character:

> Remember me, Lydia, when I am departed,
> Live over those moments when they, too, are gone;
> Be still to your minstrel the soft and kind-hearted,
> And droop o'er the marble where he lies alone.
>
> Remember how freely that heart, that to others
> Was dark as the tempest-dawn frowning above,
> Burst open to thine with the zeal of a brother's,
> And showed all its hues in the light of thy love.
>
> And, oh! in that moment when over him sighing,
> Forgive, if his failings should flash on thy brain;
> Remember, the heart that beneath thee is lying,
> Can never awake to offend thee again.
>
> And say, while ye pause on each sweet recollection,
> 'Let love like mine own on his spirit attend:
> For to me his heart turned with a poet's affection,
> Just less than a lover, and more than a friend.
>
> 'Was he selfish? – not quite; but his spirit was glowing
> With thronging affections, unanswered, unknown;
> He looked all round the world with a heart overflowing.
> But found not another to love like his own.
>
> 'Yet how? – did the worthy avoid or forsake him?
> Ah no! for Heaven blessed him with many a friend;
> But few were so trusting that might not mistake him,
> Oh, none were so dear that he could not offend!
>
> 'Yet peace to his clay in its dreary dominion,
> I know that to me he was good and sincere;
> And that Virtue ne'er shadowed, with tempering pinion,
> An honester friendship than Death covers here!'[53]

He loved her deeply, knew his case was hopeless, sublimated his feelings for her in a display of warm affection for her children, her husband and herself. When his prudishness came to the fore he felt guilty about it all and cold-shouldered his friends and subsequently repented of his churlishness. All the time, he valued Lydia and James Fisher as intelligent friends who loved his writings and provided for him a welcome oasis of culture in an intellectual desert. The two families visited each other, corresponded regularly, valued each other's friendship greatly.

Had Lydia been free to marry, how differently the whole story might have ended! The night before he left his brother's home for the last time, to join the Christian Brothers, he wrote:

I believe we both give each other credit for that strong and lively interest in all that concerns the happiness of either, without which friendship is but a name. In parting with my old desk, which has accompanied me through almost all my labours in the literature of the world, for which, perhaps, I have worked at least quite as hard as it deserved, it occurred to me that you would attach some value to what would be worthless in the eyes of most others – so I leave it for you, dear Lydia, and in it your letters, and my own hateful share of the correspondence. Of the latter, I opened one or two, and found them so odious that I was not much tempted to proceed . . . If we do meet again in this life, dear Lydia, as I hope we often may, I trust it will be with unaltered feelings of confidence and friendship. Our dear Lucy said she never knew any one so like a *real* sister as you were, and such, dear Lydia, I beg of you to continue always to me and mine. I fear you will think this letter cold, as my manner has often been, even when my feelings were farthest from indifference.[54]

It says so much, this last, sad, dismissive letter which is so clearly intended as a final severing of his ties with her. His desk is to be hers – a touching gesture certainly, but inside it are all her letters to make the gift a painful one. His letters to her are now 'hateful' and 'odious' to him. His self-disgust is so absolute that he must emphasise it by repetition. And Lucy enters the letter, in a significantly magisterial role, to define their relationship for them yet again as that of brother and sister, lest any dangerous misunderstandings should arise. Passion and duty have clashed and duty has emerged victorious but the price in frustration, pain and self-disgust has been high. It is small wonder that he could not endure to have the relationship reopened in even the most formal manner and could not bear to see her when she called later at his monastery in Dublin.

6

The last phase: the later fiction and the creative decline

In the latter part of the year 1832, Mr Moore having been invited by some of the most influential of the electors of Limerick to stand for the representation of that city, an address to him, embodying their wishes on the subject, was numerously and respectably signed. As Gerald was then about to depart for London, on one of his customary winter visits, he was requested to be the bearer of it. He asked me to accompany him, and, as such a trip promised too much pleasure to be declined, I was very glad to do so. The object of this visit failed, Mr Moore's engagements not permitting him to take advantage of the kind offer made to him; but it gave us an opportunity of enjoying, in the most favourable circumstances possible, the society of one of whom his country has such just reason to be proud.[1]

This visit, which took place late in 1832, to the most celebrated of contemporary Irish writers, was clearly an exciting occasion for Gerald Griffin. He described it in considerable detail later, in a long letter to Lydia Fisher from Taunton where he was researching the background material for his historical novel, *The Duke of Monmouth*.[2] Moore had earlier been approached by the Limerick Union, for whom Dr William Griffin had acted as spokesman, with a request that he stand as the member for Limerick.[3] A fairly lengthy correspondence ensued and a certain amount of confusion arose in regard to Moore's response to the Limerick Union's proposal. He began by informing the members of the Union that it was not financially possible for him to accede to their request and, in reply to this, they set about making him an offer of £400 a year as an inducement. Moore's letter to William Griffin, in which he rejected the request, actually reached William at his home in 48 George Street, Limerick on the evening of November 5, the very day on which Daniel and Gerald left Limerick to call on Moore. William, upset by Moore's refusal, wrote a rather angry letter to the poet but the matter was amicably concluded when Moore wrote a formal and gracious letter of refusal to the electors of Limerick.[4] Daniel O'Connell had been particularly anxious to secure Thomas Moore as candidate and had taken an active part in trying to persuade him. Moore's decision had already been made, however, by the time Gerald and Daniel Griffin came to call on him.

The brothers put up at the Castle Inn at Devizes and called on Moore at Sloperton Cottage on November 8. They were graciously received by the famous minstrel and dined with him that evening. Moore's diary contains a revealing comment on his visitors:

Was surprised by a visit from two Limerick gentlemen, the brothers of my correspondent in that city, Dr Griffin; and one of them the author of the very striking novel, 'The Collegians'. They had come, as they told me, expressly on the subject of my election for Limerick . . . Asked them to stay to dinner, which they readily agreed to do; and, though I was obliged to leave them a great deal to themselves, not being able to spare the time from my study, we had at intervals a good deal of conversation on the subject of their mission, and there certainly could not have been found two more anxious or pressing suitors . . . Talbot at dinner, and very agreeable. My Irish guests shy and silent; but Talbot and I made up the deficiency in both ways.[5]

Daniel's account of the evening and of the dinner-party confirms Moore's comment on the shyness of at least one of his Irish guests:

It was singular, though I could perceive that Gerald enjoyed himself very much during the evening, and though the gaiety and freedom of Mr Moore's manner were calculated to put all kinds of formality to flight, he could not shake off that constitutional timidity and reserve which was so apt to assail him before strangers.[6]

Later, Daniel indicates that, when Gerald and he called on Moore again the following day, the poet gently adverted to Gerald's reserve on the previous evening:

on our visit next day, when we chatted over the proceedings of the evening, and Mrs Moore said, 'But did you observe last night, what wild spirits he was in, and how he did talk? Why, I thought he was mad! I never saw anything like him.' 'Oh!' said Mr Moore, 'don't you know the meaning of that? That was,' he continued, turning playfully to Gerald, and darting his finger towards him with a good-natured smile, 'that was in order to get *you* to talk.' Gerald seemed rather taken aback by the suddenness of this gentle little reproach, but made no reply.[7]

Curiously, Gerald himself seemed to feel that he had acquired a considerable degree of social phlegm, as his conversation with his brother, on their return to their hotel, would seem to indicate:

We slept in a double-bedded room in the Castle Inn at Devizes, and before finally closing our eyes, spoke of the adventures of the day. Gerald, as he laid his head upon the pillow, said, 'Well, nothing astonished me more than the greatness of the change that has come over me. I remember the time when the bare idea – the very thought of spending such a day as this with Moore would have thrown me into such a fever, that there would not be the least chance of my sleeping a wink all night; yet, now I *have* seen him, and have spent an enchanting day with him, and yet I can lie down, not only with the most perfect certainty of delicious rest, but with a degree of calmness and quiet that I am myself astonished at.'[8]

One feels, on reading this, that Gerald's protestations merely serve to reveal the tensions he had imposed upon himself in regard to the visit to Moore. Daniel seems to share this view of Gerald's mood when he goes on to include in the *Life* Gerald's letter to Lydia from Taunton, written nearly five months later but bursting with boyish delight and pride as he describes to his dear Lydia his meeting with his boyhood idol:

Oh, dear L—, I saw the poet! and I spoke to him, and he spoke to me, and it was not to bid me 'get out of his way,' as the King of France did to the man who boasted that his majesty had spoken to him; but it was to shake hands with me, and to ask me 'How I did, Mr Griffin,' and to speak of 'my fame.' *My* fame! Tom Moore talk of my fame! Ah, the rogue! he was humbugging, L—, I'm afraid. He knew the soft side of an author's heart, and perhaps he had pity on my long, melancholy looking figure, and said to himself, 'I will make this poor fellow feel pleasant if I can,' for which, with all his roguery, who could help liking him and being grateful to him?[9]

Gerald went from Devizes to London, as he informs Lydia:

Well, then, I parted from Dan shocking lonesome, and came away to London, where Saunders and Otley set me to work for the whole winter, and after bringing three volumes to something like a conclusion it has been agreed on all sides to postpone its publication to another season.[10]

The three-volume work to which Gerald here refers must be *Tales of My Neighbourhood,* published eventually in 1835. This was to be the last collection of his tales to be published before his death. He was already preparing his last novel, *The Duke of Monmouth,* when he wrote this letter to Lydia Fisher.

Tales of My Neighbourhood (1835)

Gerald had earlier written to Lydia about the drudgery of putting together a three-volume work of fiction and this last collection of his tales bears ample witness to the strain he describes. It is a long work, a somewhat uneasy amalgam of long and short stories with interspersed narrative poems. The inclusion of these poems as separate items in the collection suggests that Griffin may have experienced some difficulty in extending the volume to the desired length. He had previously used poems only as introductory fore-pieces to his prose fictions. The collection is something of a job lot and the quality of the work varies wildly from story to story. This book contains examples of Griffin's more notable virtues and defects as a writer.

The first volume contains two stories, *The Barber of Bantry* and *The Great House.* The former, by far the longest story in the work, is in Griffin's worst manner. Excessively long, cir-cuitous, slow to get to the point, it rambles on from anecdote to anecdote, from one pointless digression to another, before the line of the main narrative emerges. This concerns the murder of a tax-gatherer named Moynehan, a crime of which the barber of the title is long suspected but which, in the end, is laid at the door of some drunken squireens. The leisurely narrative is dressed in a sauce of superstition. Fiends and apparitions of a rustically Faustian kind abound. In its detail and general tone, the narrative is sometimes reminiscent of some of the more melodramatic sections of *The Collegians.* Once again one feels the ranting shade of Edmund Kean at Griffin's elbow, prompting him to 'strong' dramatic scenes flavoured with melodrama and superstition. Yet, as with the earlier and more famous novel, there is here also a solid base of closely observed and effectively rendered detail of a realistic

kind. Behind all the fustian there is a lively and interesting Irish
world of small tradesmen and cobblers, barbers and pedlars,
shopkeepers and farmers, shading upwards into the 'half-quality'
of Tipsy Castle and Castle Tobin. Melodramatic sonorities
unexpectedly taper off into lively and convincing rustic humour.
Structurally, however, the story is altogether a lamentable
performance for a writer of Griffin's experience.

Very much more successful is *The Great House*, an amusing
short story in which Peter Guerin, a village shopkeeper, is
asked to dine at the local mansion in return for some kindness
done by his family to the younger brother of the local squire,
Lord Peppercorn. The story is narrated directly by Guerin
himself who innocently sets off at noon to walk the four miles
to the Great House. He spends two hours sitting in the lodge
gate-house under the mistaken impression that this is the mansion proper. When he finally reaches the Great House itself it is
three o'clock in the afternoon and he is astonished to hear that
the ladies and 'jettlemen' do not propose to dine until seven. He
has been fasting since eight o'clock that morning and is more
than ready for dinner when it finally arrives. By constantly
inviting him to take wine with them, the gentlemen effectively
prevent him from eating any of the many courses served. He
watches course after course being removed by the staff and
finally delights the company by drinking two finger-bowls full
of water. Later, in the drawing-room, he adds to their amusement by showing the ladies his latest pattern-book and soliciting
orders. The visit provides ceaseless amusement for the company
and Peter Guerin returns home hungry and resolved never to
dine with the great again.

The story is an effectively controlled exposure of the cruel
abuse of Peter's rustic innocence. His own voice is used for the
narration of the incidents and the nastiness of the 'great' is
revealed throughout. Peter remains ignorant of the cruel joke
that has been played on him to the very end. His dialogue is
competently devised, at once amusing and engaging. This is
the side of Griffin's talent which was to be so warmly commended
by Edith Somerville, who clearly enjoyed his control of rustic
speech.[11] The writers of the 'R.M.' stories would have found
much to enjoy in this little comic story and would surely have

appreciated the full force of its amiable satire, displayed in such
scenes as the following, in which Peter recounts his first encounter with the mysterious finger-bowls:

> There I sat, a'most dead. 'What'll they bring in next, I wondher,'
> says I. 'Twasn't long until I seen 'em comin' an' layin' before every
> one at table a great big glass o' could spring wather. 'Cool comfort,
> Pether,' says I – 'but here goes for manners.' So I drank it off. When
> the jettleman seen I dhrank it, he fill'd it again, an' if he did, I
> dhrank it again to plase him; but seein' he was goin' to fill it again, I
> couldn't stand it any longer. 'No more o' that Sir,' says I, 'if you
> plase.' Well, I thought they never would stop laughin'. But, Molly,
> I thought the sighth would be took out o' my two eyes, when I seen
> all the ladies and jettlemen dippin' their hands in their glasses, an'
> washin' 'em before my face at the dinner table! 'Well, Peter,' says I,
> 'such manners as that you never seen before this day any way.'[12]

The contrast between rustic naiveté and Big-House condescension is achieved with fine economy in a racy narrative notably
devoid of the appalling longueurs which disfigure the preceding
tale. It is, perhaps, significant that Griffin achieves this kind
of force and power on this particular subject, the baiting of
an Irish innocent by a collection of semi-Anglicised half-
gentry.

Volume II contains three stories and a poem: *A Night at Sea*;
Touch My Honour, Touch My Life; *Sir Dowling O'Hartigan*; *The
Nightwalker*.

A Night at Sea is rather a long story and, like the other longer
items in this book, would have benefited from sharp pruning.
In so far as it has a main theme, it could be said to concern the
effects of an excessively liberal education on the young. Griffin
not infrequently adverts to conflicting notions on the education
of the young and is himself quite clearly sceptical of the unduly
permissive approach of theorists like Rousseau who advocate
giving the young their head. In this story, Major O'Connor
allows his daughter to run on a loose rein, permitting her to
read whatever she fancies and generally indulging her whims.
She repays him by eloping with a poor suitor and her furious
father refuses to see her ever again. He is finally reconciled with
her by his grandchild. The narrative is slack and leisurely but,
along the way, we are presented with an amusing picture of
Irish small-town life with its local jealousies and animosities.

The moralising narrative fails to hold our attention but we are occasionally entertained by the scenery and the characters.

Touch My Honour, Touch My Life is a piously serious attack on the vogue for duelling which obtained in a slightly earlier phase of Irish history. The violent practices of the Hell-Fire Club are glanced at disapprovingly and we are presented with a sad story of two dear friends who become embroiled in a duel as a result of the silly code of honour fashionable in their regiment. The death of one leaves the other sorely smitten by life-long remorse and it is something of a relief both to him and to the reader when he dies heroically abroad during active service. Once again, the narrative is excruciatingly moral but there is an entirely hilarious portrait of a rustic Irish dancing master, one Thady Houlahan, who marvellously unfits his pupils for the polite measures of the metropolis. Thady, along with the schoolmaster, Theophilus O'Gallagher, proves some compensation for the tedium of the main narrative. Here is Thady instructing young Ulick O'Connor in the secrets of the dance:

Now, Mr Ulick! Hould up your head, sir, and show what you can do. Cut three times now before you come to the ground – very good! Once again – higher – higher! Don't come down yet – Ah, sir, I am teaching you to dance and not to walk – What business have you of two feet on the ground together? One would fancy you were in the hands of those city dancin' masters, who teach their pupils to go one–two–three – one–two–three, about a room as cautiously as if the floor were strewed with new-laid eggs. Make it a maxim, Mr Ulick, from the time you get up to dance till you sit down again, never to let the two feet touch the floor together for a second; and the longer you can keep both in the air the better. Now – spring off the ball o' the foot – that's it – higher! Ah, fie for shame, sir, one would think you were going on with one of those *minutes*, as they call 'em, where a man might as well be following a funeral – for any real dancing that's in 'em. Now, sir, cut three times! Stay up! Don't come down awhile! Ah, but you have come down to some purpose.[13]

Ulick comes down to such 'purpose' that he gives himself a bloody nose and has to be conveyed from the field of battle. One such rumbustious, comic scene is worth acres of the tedious preaching which accompanies it in these later tales.

Sir Dowling O'Hartigan is a short, historical fable set in the time of the Battle of Clontarf. Sir Dowling is one of King Brien's

knights who is called to do battle against the Danes. He encounters a crone who presents him with a magic cloak which
renders him invisible to his enemies. Protected by this, he does
prodigies in the battle but, hearing his name called by Brien's
son, removes the cloak and is killed instantly. It is a slight tale
which was to be later reprinted in the posthumous collection,
Talis Qualis or Tales of the Jury Room (1842).

The Nightwalker is a narrative poem which tells the sad story
of the fate of one of those unhappy beings about whom Gerald
had written so disapprovingly to Lydia from Taunton a few
years earlier. The 'nightwalker' of the poem is a young man
who is enticed into joining a band of 'moonlighters', midnight
terrorists who are bent on assaulting a local castle. They are
betrayed to the soldiery by the very one who had led them on
to their dark deeds and are captured and banished to Van
Diemen's Land. Griffin's voice is heard clearly in the following
stanza:

> O, you who bless these dawning skies
> In yon receding vales,
> Take warning from my parting sighs,
> And from those swelling sails!
> To answer crime with crime is worse
> Than tamely to endure;
> And ev'n for black oppression's curse
> Dark treason is no cure.[14]

Although he is never openly sympathetic to such figures in his
fiction, his novels and stories exhibit considerable understanding
of the vile social and political conditions which drove an
unhappy peasantry to such desperate expedients.

Volume III contains eight short stories and two long poems.
A brief account of each of these will suffice to give some idea of
the range of the material and the degree of the writer's success.

The Village Ruin, like the earlier story, *Sir Dowling O'Hartigan*, is a brief, historical fable of no great complexity. This time,
the setting is the Ireland we have already been introduced to
in the long novel, *The Invasion*. Thorgills, the Viking leader, has
conquered and shamed the Irish king, O'Melachlin. He adds
insult to injury by demanding the king's daughter, the virtuous
Melcha. Spurred into action at last, the king devises a plan

whereby the Vikings are defeated and thwarted of their prey. Melcha behaves with great courage and becomes a symbol of Irish resolution. She finally retires into a convent. For the moment, Ireland is free of the yoke of the Vikings, though the story makes it clear that they retain control of the sea-ports and will later reassert their power.

Shanid Castle is a narrative poem in sixty-five stanzas, celebrating the greatness of the Geraldine Earls of Desmond. Shanid Castle is betrayed to the enemy and the Countess of Desmond done to death in the ensuing struggle but a Desmond eventually returns in triumph to reclaim his heritage from the son of the traitor.

The Cavern is a brief, allegorical exercise in which the narrator descends into a cave where he encounters various apparitions. His guide is a 'Printer's Devil' and he encounters such personages as Duel, Suicides, Disease, Hypocrisy, before managing to escape to the upper air. The tone is mildly satirical but the satire lacks any real focus. Too many targets are presented and the story is too short to do justice to them all.

The Force of Conscience is a highly moral tale of a rural murder and an old beggarman who is arrested and hanged for the murder, having been convicted erroneously on circumstantial evidence. One of the real murderers is guilt-stricken and eventually confesses and pays the penalty. The unreliability of circumstantial evidence is a theme on which Griffin frequently harps.

The Sun-Stroke, a short tale, set in the period of the Insurrection of 1798, tells of twin brothers who become embroiled in a plot based on love and jealousy. The story is told with fair economy and force and a real sense of the desperate and troubled period permeates it. The deranged brother, Lewy, is an effective vehicle for humour and pathos. *The Sun-Stroke* has a sense of form lacking in many of the other tales.

Send the Fool Farther, almost an 'R.M.' story, describes the career of a practical joker, one Captain Bounce, who has the tables turned on him by a conspiracy of his victims and fails to relish the experience.

Mount Orient, another one of the more amusing tales, gaily pillories a vulgar family of pretentious half-gentry. At the centre of the stage is the splendid Miss Mimosa M'Orient who professes the most charitable and patriotic sentiments while, simultaneously, driving Irish beggars from her door. She is delightfully depicted and we rejoice in her comic overthrow in the proposal scene where she imagines that the eligible Mr Fitzpatrick is wooing her elegant self when, in fact, he has come in pursuit of her plainer, less showy relative, Miss de Courcy. The amiable satire is pleasantly and lightly handled and the serious message about Ireland's poor, which underlies the flimsy story, is, for once, ably implied rather than stressed.

Orange and Green is a short and sentimental ballad in which the conflict between Orange and Green is improbably resolved.

The Philanthropist is a mildly fantastic story in which Griffin achieves a comic success. The philanthropist of the title is Mr Everard Sweetman who founds an ill-fated, educational academy for the dissemination of his advanced views. Once again, as in the earlier story, *A Night at Sea*, excessive liberalism in education is being attacked but the attack this time is through comedy and, accordingly, more palatable. Everard Sweetman develops, in the course of the story, into a sort of Celtic Walter Mitty who plunges his family into debt in order to pay for his experiments and runs away from home to pursue his theories. His doings are recounted in a spirit of fun and this slight and amusing story reveals in Griffin a real talent for comic absurdity.

The Blackbirds and the Yellow Hammers, the concluding story, is a mixture of knockabout rural farce and folk legend. The blackbirds and yellow hammers of the title are two factions whose hilariously violent doings are interwoven with a slight love story. Once again, as so often in Griffin's work, the chaos of the society is exposed. The warring factions are described to us in a manner which places the blame for their existence where it belongs:

They might, it is true, have been better off if they had been better educated; but they were too poor to educate themselves, and unhappily their superiors, being of a different religion, could not be brought to afford them gratuitous instruction, unmingled with danger to their faith, which the peasantry were not willing to surrender. No other field, therefore, being open to the exercise of his active mind, and no other subject afforded on which his ardent temperament might exhaust itself with utility, or even without evil, it is no wonder that honest Paddy, in our neighbourhood, as in other parts of the island, for lack of better employment, took to whiskey and glory![15]

The faction fight which climaxes the story is an odd mixture of brutality and hilarity, with members of the rival factions killing and maiming each other while, at the same time, leading the military, who have intervened, a merry dance through bog and briar.

Unsatisfactory as *Tales of My Neighbourhood* may be in the many respects indicated, it does, nevertheless, convey a genuine sense of the chaos of Griffin's times and, at its best, manages to do so quite entertainingly. This flawed book reflects the struggle between his fine comic gift and the moral pedantry which was its greatest foe. Artistically flawed though it is, it gives us a genuine sense of the place and its many people. The book has a modest place in a line which eventually flowers into Moore's *The Untilled Field* and Joyce's *Dubliners*. An effort is made to link the stories by allowing occasional characters to reappear from story to story. The series of tales is by no means altogether lacking in art and the range of effects is considerable. There is enough successful social satire in the book to make one regret Griffin's decline into a tragic, aesthetic *simplesse*. Of the extent of this decline his next work, his last novel, was to afford distressing evidence.

The Duke of Monmouth (1836)

Why Griffin should have gone to an episode in English history for the material for his next work is not clear. Daniel's biography affords no clues to this. The letter to Lydia in which Gerald had given his delighted account of his visit to Moore is dated March 31, 1833 and, in the course of it, he mentions that he has been at Taunton 'the greater part of the time since before Christmas', which would seem to indicate that he took some pains to familiarise himself with the locality in which his novel was to be based. A remark of Daniel's confirms that Gerald took great care with his last novel: '*The Duke of Monmouth* was almost the only one of his later writings into the subject of which he made some effort, as in *The Collegians*, though after much persuasion, to fling himself with the devotion of a deep interest.'[16] The novel itself is a fairly competent example of its kind, combining in the manner of this *genre* a tragic love story with the depiction of the violent historical events. Griffin may have been moved to the attempt by his admiration for John Banim's long historical novel, *The Boyne Water* (1826), about which he had written to his sister, Ellen, when it was first published.[17] His own work is a good deal less tedious than Banim's leisurely story, though it resembles it in its employment of the familiar device of drawing its pair of lovers from opposite camps. Aquila Fullerton espouses the cause of the rebel Duke of Monmouth, while her betrothed, Henry Kingsley, is a soldier in the army of King James. Monmouth's rebellion is depicted competently and rapidly. In fact, the general efficiency of the performance would seem to confirm Daniel's judgement on the care Gerald took with this last novel.

One detail of the plot, however, caused him considerable distress and his handling of it reveals the extent to which he had begun to allow the moralist in him to overrule the writer. The incident in question concerns the heroine, Aquila Fullerton. Early in the story, she has been made to repulse the unwelcome advances of the unpleasant Colonel Kirke. After Monmouth's defeat and execution, Kirke and Judge Jeffreys set out on their dreadful trail of vengeance in the West Country. Kirke arrests both Aquila Fullerton and her brother, Arthur. Lust and wounded vanity combine to make him offer Aquila her brother's freedom at the price of her honour. This was, in fact, an incident from real life but, in the real-life version Kirke, having had his way with the girl, ordered the execution of the brother nevertheless. Daniel Griffin records Gerald's dislike of this incident and his inability to absorb it straight into his fiction:

He was a long time at a loss how to manage the plot of this tale, the historical fact as regarded the heroine, and the infamous cruelty of Colonel Kirke in the most harrowing incident of it, being of too revolting a nature to be made use of in a work of fiction; the difficulty being, that any alteration made to lessen the horror of the transaction, would, besides being historically incorrect, tend to diminish the infamy of that fiendish character, and therefore weaken the interest of the whole scene by placing the heroine in a more honourable position. He, however, eventually contrived to manage the matter without lessening the reader's sympathy for the sufferer, preserving her reputation by a marriage, which to her persecutor was only one of convenience.[18]

In the novel, in fact, Aquila is 'married' to Kirke by a demented preacher who is forced to enact a mockery of a wedding ceremony which, clearly, could not have fooled a child, let alone the practical young woman Aquila Fullerton has shown herself to be. She has, earlier in the story, been depicted as an emancipated and ardent supporter of Monmouth who argues with her lover and his loyal sister and actually stops Monmouth in the streets of Taunton in order to present to him some new colours she has woven for him. To suggest that she could have been taken in by the absurd stratagem devised by the prudish Griffin is utter nonsense. He preserves his heroine's reputation to the detriment of his fiction and does so, in any case, quite unnecessarily by any standards one cares to apply. The incident is sadly trivial and it is embarrassingly revelatory of the dire pass to which this writer had come at this late stage of his career.

THE LAST YEARS

The *Life* does not provide very exhaustive coverage of Griffin's last years, except in regard to the tour of Scotland which he undertook with Daniel in April and May of 1838.[19] It is clear that Griffin's thoughts had been turning more and more to the religious life. His sisters, Lucy and Anna, had already entered convents and he was deeply saddened by the death of his beloved cousin, Matt, in India in 1837. Something of the sombreness of his mood at this stage can be gathered from the lengthy letter he wrote to Lucy about Matt's death.[20] He paid his last visit to London in 1835 and, towards the end of the following year, surprised his family by making a mysterious visit to France. The purpose and precise destination of this visit remain a secret to the present day. Gerald simply disappeared one day and was not heard of again for three weeks, when finally a letter reached his family bearing the Calais post-mark. This letter apparently contained some directions about his works and gave no clue to the purpose of his visit to France. He had frequently talked of visiting France in former years and had mentioned to Lucy when writing to her from Taunton that he sometimes took walks with an old French priest there. Daniel and the rest of the family appear to have thought that he might have gone to St Omers to pursue a course of study but, if the account in the *Life* is to be trusted, the family seem to have behaved with remarkable restraint and discretion, refraining from badgering him for further information about his trip. On his return, he resumed his life of regular study and devotion and appears to have spent the year 1837 quietly at home. He had once discussed with Daniel the possibility of his having a vocation for the priesthood but he appears to have decided at this time that he had been mistaken in this.

In April 1838 Daniel persuaded him to go on a three-week trip to Scotland which they both enjoyed. Daniel includes in the *Life* sizeable extracts from the notebook which Gerald kept of the trip and they make lively and entertaining reading.[21] The trip seems to have had the effect of causing him to cast aside his cares for a while. At any rate, he clearly enjoyed the travel and the sightseeing hugely. His comments on his fellow-passengers are detailed and vivid. His novelist's eye was clearly hard at work on the journey by canal-boat which began the trip and he is satirical at his own expense when he weeps for Robert Burns while passing what he takes for the Ayrshire coast and later discovers that he has been wasting his romantic tears on the coast of Wigton. Glasgow, Edinburgh, Stirling and Holyrood were all visited and Scotland's mountains and lakes duly exclaimed over. The travellers walked through the Trossachs and boated on Loch Katrine and Loch Lomond. They returned to Ireland in high spirits and arrived back in Limerick on May 10.

In August Gerald informed his family of his intention of joining the Christian Brothers' teaching Order and his astonished family produced a reaction of which the redoubtable Simon Dedalus himself might well have been proud:

We heard this announcement with the utmost regret; in fact, it would not be easy to describe our feelings when it was first disclosed to us. Though our unilluminated perceptions might have made us lament his desertion of literature, there were many things to reconcile us to the life of a clergyman if he had adopted it. The vast practical good effected in the ministry; the chance that by his talents or his future writings he might shed a lustre upon the church, and become one of its standing ornaments (ideas, many of them worldly in their origin, and allied to pride and vanity, but still not unnatural); all these things influenced us in favour of that mode of life; but that a person with abilities of the highest order should leave the world, and set himself down to such a simple task as the instruction of the poor – a task which any one, we thought, could easily execute – it seemed to us like the degrading of most excellent faculties from their sphere, and devoting them to very unworthy purposes. Besides this, we were informed that many members of this society were men of humble origin, and that they would be totally incapable of appreciating Gerald's talents, or his habits of feeling and of thought.[22]

Daniel goes on, however, to record his newly-won conviction that the family's assumptions about the new teaching Order had been quite unjustified. He pays handsome tribute to the society's aims and to the kindness shown to his troubled brother. Gerald entered the novitiate at North Richmond Street, Dublin on September 8, 1838 and, when called upon to select a new name as a Brother, chose 'Joseph'. Typically, he seems to have embarked on his new career with intense dedication, abandoning his literary work entirely and giving himself to a scrupulously exact performance of his religious and teaching duties. He was admitted to the religious habit on the feast of St Teresa, October 15, just over a month after his entry to the Order and embarked on a two-year novitiate. It would be five years before it would be necessary for him to commit himself to the taking of final vows.

Daniel Griffin's understandably tender account of this phase of his brother's life makes it almost painfully clear that Gerald took with him into his new career all the excessively demanding moral scrupulosity and perfectionism which had already wreaked such havoc on his creative instincts. When he was at first permitted to sleep in an apartment by himself he hastened to the spiritual director to ask that no discrimination be applied in his case and that he be permitted to sleep in the common dormitory. When this request had been granted he then became worried in case his action smacked of disobedience and an unwillingness to submit his will to that of the director. Accordingly, he returned to the director and asked him to issue commands without regard to Gerald's own feelings in the matter. On this occasion and on all others of a similar kind his religious advisers seem to have acted with great tact and understanding to which Daniel pays grateful tribute. This was particularly true in regard to the novelist's determination to abandon his writing career entirely:

From the moment he had fairly entered on his new mode of life, he manifested the greatest disinclination to take a pen in his hand; he could not bear the idea of it; it seemed as if he shrank with an avoidance almost amounting to loathing, from an employment to which he had long been indebted for much mental suffering. He used to tell a story of a painter, of uncommon genius, who had entered a religious community, and who had destroyed his palettes and brushes, lest they should afterwards prove an occasion of temptation, and it seems not improbable that he applied this lesson to himself. I could not help admiring the judgement which the members of the community displayed in their management of him in this respect: they did not, in the least, urge him upon the subject, but left him altogether to himself.[23]

This tolerant and understanding approach seems to have had the desired effect, and towards the end of his life the writer's distaste for his earlier vocation seems to have been allayed to the extent that he was willing to undertake the composition of a few tales of a pious nature.

He seems to have welcomed the austerities of his new life and to have fitted well into his new surroundings. Daniel describes his daily regimen in some detail. Gerald would rise at five, spend an hour in prayer, read a spiritual lecture and then attend Mass. He breakfasted at eight and subsequently taught in the school until midday. There followed another hour of spiritual exercises and two further hours of teaching. After a meal he then permitted himself some conversation with his fellow Brothers and the later part of the day would be spent in study and recreation. He was, it seems, often called on to sing a song during the evening recreation period and appeared happy to oblige. Daniel appears to have kept in touch with his brother and cheerful letters to William, Daniel and Lucy have survived in the archives of the Christian Brothers. In one of these Gerald describes at length a visit he paid to his sister, Anna, who had entered the Order of the Sisters of Charity.[24] The account he gives Lucy of this outing is lively and apparently serene but Daniel reveals in the *Life* that the meeting with Anna affected Gerald so deeply that he could never again be persuaded to repeat the visit.[25] Thus, it would seem that Lydia Fisher was not quite alone in experiencing this kind of rejection. Gerald appears to have been desperately determined to avoid as much as possible the renewal of old contacts and the reopening of painful associations.

In June 1839 he was transferred to the Cork house of his Order, at the North Monastery, where he continued to teach and to practise his chosen spiritual life. The Christian Brothers were at this time engaged in the production of their first set of school books and Gerald appears to have helped with the editing of these and to have contributed some of his own works to the new volumes, as he rather coyly indicates in a letter to his sister, Lucy, in November 1839:

The C. Brothers are just about publishing a reading book for our schools – and for yours if you wish to introduce it – there is some nice poetry in it by a Cork contributor (no acquaintance of yours however, notwithstanding that knowing smile you gave just now) also some delicious lines to a *Canary Bird* which probably you will recognise.[26]

A later passage in the same letter provides poignant evidence that memories could still come to torment him even in the peace and seclusion of a monastery:

Sometimes on a fine day here I get lonesome thoughts and I think if we were all in poor Pallas again, how much more worthy I would strive to make myself of all the happiness and all the affection which was lavished on me in that dear little village – how many things I would not do that I did, and how many things I would do that I left undone – how different I would be altogether from what I was and then experience and common sense come in and tell me that it is a waste of thought and that I would be again previously what I was and that it would be much wiser to apply one's care to the present than to be mentally repairing a miserable past that is already far away and that all the thinking in the world cannot now make one whit better or worse.[27]

Daniel called to see him in September and got permission to take Gerald to visit his favourite sister, Lucy, at the Presentation Convent in Youghal:

The day was beautiful: we took outside seats on the coach, and he was in the highest spirits. We had several conversations about literature, and literary people, all his old recollections seemed to revive, and he spoke on these subjects with an ardour and warmth of expression that quite surprised me, yet with a degree of calmness that

showed that they were now no longer capable of disturbing his peace.
I remember, particularly, his speaking with great enthusiasm of some
of the scenes in Woodstock, especially of that beautiful one, Crom-
well's soliloquy before the picture. We returned to the monastery
early in the evening, and he resumed his studies with his usual
energy.[28]

This would seem to suggest that literary enthusiasm was far
from completely dead, in spite of his purposeful asceticism.

He was, in fact, engaged on the story, *The Holy Island*,
towards the end of his life. One evening, when he was at work
on it, the dinner bell rang. With characteristic obedience he laid
down his pen in mid-sentence, never to take it up again. He had
suffered in April 1840 a sharp, feverish attack of a kind to which
he had been subject years before and during the month of May
he wrote to his brother, Dr William Griffin, to ask his advice
about attacks of palpitations and nervous strain. He appeared
to be making a slow recovery but, on June 10, the Superior
wrote to the Griffin family to tell them that Gerald had been
ill for some days and that he appeared to be suffering from a
fever. Daniel hastened to Cork to find his younger brother dying
of typhus fever and sinking fast. As Daniel informed Lucy by
letter shortly afterwards, Gerald could scarcely recognise him:

I asked him to put out his tongue which he could not & then I asked
him 'Do you know me Gerald?' He said, 'No, Dan' – I ran into the
next room to write the note to William and the nurse told me that
when I went out of the room he said – where is he? – but there was a
great stupor on him and he never seemed to take any notice of me
again which made me sorry afterwards that I did not then try to
rouse him and get him if possible to speak a little – for an hour or
two after that he seemed to improve in some of his symptoms which
made me hope against appearances. Indeed they were such that I
would have been quite in despair of any other in the same state, but
it was so hard to believe it – He never said any thing I could understand afterwards except once that he was tossing and restless I
asked him if he wished to get out of bed? and he said but very
indistinctly – 'not immediately'.[29]

He died early on the morning of June 12 and was buried on
June 15 in the community's graveyard, attached to the North
Monastery. A plain headstone names him as Brother Gerald
Joseph Griffin and gives his age as thirty-six years.

7

Posthumous publications and Griffin's literary significance

Daniel Griffin, who appears to have been his brother's literary executor, has left no account of his handling of Gerald's literary remains or of the preparation of the *Life and Works of Gerald Griffin* (1842–43). The variations between the *Life and Works* and the first editions have been remarked in the Textual Note. As Sadleir indicates, the prospectus of the *Life and Works* announced twelve volumes but only eight eventually appeared.[1] Two posthumous publications are deserving of notice, the three-volume collection of tales, *Talis Qualis or Tales of the Jury Room*, first published in 1842, and the play, *Gisippus*, on which Griffin had once built such high hopes and which was eventually produced by Macready in 1842.

Talis Qualis or Tales of the Jury Room (1842)

Since it is known that Griffin did no professional writing after he entered the Christian Brothers in 1838 it is not now possible to do more than speculate about the provenance of the stories in this collection. As has been noted in Chapter 6, one of them, *Sir Dowling O'Hartigan*, was taken from *Tales of My Neighbourhood* (1835), and the fact that it was found necessary to make up the total in the posthumous volume by the inclusion of a story already published so recently suggests various possibilities. It suggests first that, if the volume was planned by Griffin himself, he must have left it in an unfinished state. Alternatively, *Talis Qualis* may have been planned by someone other than Griffin as a repository for a final set of those unpublished stories which Daniel had managed to collect.

The plan of the volume is endearingly improbable, involving

an English visitor to Ireland in a sort of Hibernian pastiche of *The Canterbury Tales*. He arrives in a town in the south of Ireland during the assizes and wanders into the empty jury-room at the court-house. The case at trial is a breach-of-promise and, while the visitor wanders about the jury-room, the case concludes and the jurors arrive to begin their attempts to reach a verdict. The visitor has to conceal himself in a cupboard to escape discovery and is subsequently unable to escape. The jurors fail to reach a unanimous decision and are locked in for the night. They manage to buy some oysters and ale from a passing oyster-vendor and settle down to pass the long night by telling stories and singing songs. The Foreman is made to act as chairman and empowered to exact a fine of a shilling from any member of the company who fails to oblige the party with a story and a song. This leads to the telling of the tales themselves, with the Foreman offering the first tale, *Sigismund*. The twelve stories follow one another in the manner arranged, with occasional variations supplied by one or two of the jurors who cannot sing and must pay the fine agreed upon. Sometimes too, the direct progress from one story to the next is varied by a brief discussion of the sort of material which will be acceptable to the company. When the twelfth story has been told, the listener in the cupboard betrays his presence by a sneeze, is hauled forth and made to explain himself and pay the penalty for his presence by telling a story. When he has obliged, they lower him through the window and he returns safely to his hotel. On the next day, when the jurors return to court to inform the judge that they have still failed to agree upon a verdict, the affair is brought to a suitably hilarious conclusion when the court is informed that the pair involved in the action have made up their differences and have eloped together to the Lakes of Killarney, having been married by special licence.

Once the initial improbabilities have been got over, the whole thing bowls along merrily enough. Some of the stories are clearly Griffin's and are recognisable as such by the choice of theme and the treatment given to it. The stranger's own tale, for example, which concludes the series, is a typical rendering of an historical fable about the Geraldines which recalls the long poem, *Shanid Castle*, in *Tales of My Neighbourhood*. The tale assigned to the eleventh juror, *The Prophecy*, can safely be assigned to Griffin also. It is in his manner and exhibits his familiar preoccupation with the unreliability of circumstantial evidence in courts of law. *Sir Dowling O'Hartigan*, which we know as Griffin's already, is assigned to the twelfth juror as the last of the series proper. About some of the other stories it is not easy to feel the same confidence that they came from Griffin's pen. The eighth juryman's tale, *Mr Tibbot O'Leary, The Curious*, is briskly satirical and not in the least reminiscent of Griffin's gentler, more leisurely manner. The comedy of this story recalls Carleton rather than the troubled work done by Griffin in his later period. The stories of the third and fourth jurors (*The Knight Without Reproach* and *The Mistake*) also differ in a number of respects from Griffin's normal style. The vivacity of *The Mistake* is of a kind he scarcely achieved at his most jocund and, if it is his at all, must surely date from an earlier period of his life. Certainty in these matters is impossible now in the absence of concrete evidence which is unlikely to emerge at this late stage but internal evidence repeatedly suggests the presence of an alien hand in this posthumous volume.

Gisippus (1842)

With the play, *Gisippus*, no such problems arise and its considerable interest derives from the light it throws on its author's preoccupation with a particular type of character, and from the sad irony which surrounds its eventual successful London production by the very actor-manager who had dashed Griffin's earliest dramatic hopes by his rejection of the lost play, *Aguire*, in 1823. The actress, Fanny Kelly, had expressed interest in *Gisippus* during Griffin's London period. When he sent her the first two acts of the play, she appears to have expressed warm approval of them and he then sent her acts three and four:

He at one time sent the first and second acts to Miss Kelly, who was struck with the genius they displayed, and said if the remainder of the piece was equal to what she had read, she would present it at Drury Lane for him, and that she had little doubt of being able to get it brought out. Much gratified with this unexpected kindness, Gerald sent her successively the third and fourth acts. With these she professed herself equally well pleased, and awaited some time for the fifth, but she never received it. When he had attained what he so anxiously sought for – the approval and interest of one of the most popular actresses of the day, who had full interest to get his drama attentively considered – he showed an unaccountable reluctance to avail himself of the kindness, and in fact finally left London without doing so.[2]

William Griffin, whose account this is, ascribes his brother's failure to persevere with the connection with Fanny Kelly to 'a degree of sensitiveness with respect to patronage, that made him recoil from even the ordinary and necessary means of obtaining attention for his pieces'. *Gisippus*, however, remained very dear to him and he preserved it at the end, even when he destroyed so much else. Daniel notes: 'It was singular, and perhaps indicated some lingering remains of his ancient affection for the drama, that amid all this havoc he preserved *Gisippus*, which he had then in his possession, and which he handed to his brother, Dr Griffin, when the fate of the other manuscripts was sealed.'[3]

Daniel sold the play to Macready for £300 a few months after Gerald's death and it was put on at Drury Lane in February 1842 with Macready and Helen Faucit in the leading roles. Macready's diary records the reception given to the play:

February 23rd: Acted Gisippus, I must admit, not well – not finished; not like a great actor. The actor was lost in the manager. The effect of the play was success, but I am not satisfied. I hope I shall be able, if I escape severe handling in this instance, to be more careful in future. Was called for, and very warmly received.[4]

In the summer of the same year Macready travelled to Dublin where he included Griffin's play in his repertoire for the season. He seemed happier with his performance this time:

Dublin, May 30th – Went to theatre, rehearsed Gisippus, very very wearied. Wrote a short note to Catherine. Rested, felt wearied even to illness. Acted Gisippus better than I have ever yet done, so well that I think, if I could have given the same truth and effect to it the first night in London, it must have attracted; and yet who can say? Called for and very well received.[5]

The play seems to have enjoyed some critical approval but to have made no money for Drury Lane or Macready.

It is a five-act drama in solemn blank verse about a Greek, Gisippus, and his friend, a Roman named Fulvius. Gisippus is betrothed to Sophronia but, when he discovers that she has loved Fulvius in the past and parted from him through a misunderstanding, Gisippus instantly resigns her to Fulvius. Gisippus' fortunes immediately decline, his debtors come upon him and he looks to Fulvius to save him from ruin. Fulvius is called away to Rome and Gisippus is left to face his creditors and his enemies, convinced that his friend has played him false and resolved never to trust a friend again. He is sold into slavery and, meanwhile, Fulvius is prospering in Rome and is gradually being corrupted by his success. Finally, the two friends are reconciled through Sophronia, after a series of misunderstandings and unhappy chances.

In a letter to his mother, written while he was still resident in London about fifteen years earlier, Griffin had told her of the circumstances under which the play was written and had analysed the character of Gisippus in an intriguing fashion:

Here I give you what I believe you have never had anything of – a specimen of my tragedy writing. The drama I have written since I came to London. You'd laugh if you saw how it was got through. I wrote it all in coffee houses, and on little slips of paper, from which I afterwards copied it out ... Gisippus I have made a fellow of exquisite susceptibility, almost touching on weakness; a hero in soul, but plagued with an excessive nervousness of feeling, which induces him to almost anticipate unkindness, and of course drives him frantic, when he finds it great and real – at least apparently so.[6]

This is, of course, an extraordinarily apt description not merely of Gisippus but of Gerald Griffin himself. It recalls his sad misunderstanding with John Banim, which poisoned so many of those dreary early days in London when he sorely needed a friend and Banim was more than willing to help if Griffin's prickly sensitivity had only permitted. It recalls too his continuing interest in this type of character throughout all his subsequent prose fictions, leading to Eugene Hamond in *The Half-Sir*, Hardress Cregan in *The Collegians* and Kenric in *The Invasion*. That he should have been putting this character into his plays and stories from the very beginning, without ever managing to come to grips with the ruinous defects in his own character and temperament takes us to the very heart of Griffin's personal mystery and warns of the inevitability of his eventual collapse as a creative artist. He put himself on paper again and again in circumstances which exposed the futility of his own most obvious characteristics and yet went on alienating friends, from Banim to James Fisher, suspecting coldness where none existed, recoiling from imagined slights and, every now and again, repenting warmly of his follies. Perhaps if brother William had read *Gisippus* with the proper sort of attention to the characterisation, he might not have been so surprised that his ambitious and perverse younger brother failed to send that fifth act to Fanny Kelly. He could have found the explanation in the play itself.

GRIFFIN'S LITERARY SIGNIFICANCE

Though flawed, Griffin's achievement is considerable and, to be fairly judged, must be set against the background of a peculiar temperament aggravated by a frustrating historical situation. His career, furthermore, presages much that is representative in the Anglo-Irish literary experience. He was born into an Ireland which inflicted upon him, in their most acute form, all the typical pressures of the Anglo-Irish situation. The native language was beginning to decline. The country was still wincing, politically and economically, in the aftermath of a savage Penal Code. A Catholic middle class was only just beginning to emerge and assert its claim to educational and civic freedom. Ireland had recently lost a capital city, when Dublin lost her Parliament in 1800. The period is, in many respects, unfriendly to the talents of an aspiring young Catholic writer. The horrors of the 1798 Insurrection and of Emmet's futile fling are only recently over. There is anti-climax in the national life and the society lacks all coherence. The era is one of terrorist outrage and the rapid erosion of an irresponsible Ascendancy. With Rackrents at one end of the social scale and Whiteboys at the other, these were difficult times for an ordinary citizen with a modicum of talent and a distaste for violence. Griffin's intense ambition to succeed in the drama brought about his early departure for London, the inevitable literary capital of nine-teenth-century Ireland. It made him one of the first in a long line of talented, literary exiles and his tribulations were to become almost characteristic of the type. The splendid naiveté of his grandiose ambition to reform the London stage looks forward to the arrogant programme of a more illustrious successor who modestly proposed merely to forge the conscience of his race.

To mention Griffin and Joyce in the same sentence may seem, at first, a merely whimsical conjunction and yet there are many similarities between these two, both in their circumstances and in their experiences. Each was the son of an unsuccessful, Micawberish business-man of the Catholic middle class. They were both born to town life, given a rigidly Catholic education and both were painfully ambitious of literary fame. Both wrote some excellent lyric verse, well worth preserving (Tennyson was an ardent admirer of Griffin's lovely *Aileen Aroon*). Each produced a single play which had little success during the writer's lifetime but rather more after his death. *Exiles* was one of the successes of the 1971 London season and Griffin's *Gisippus* had a *succès d'estime* at Drury Lane in 1842. Griffin and Joyce both underwent a religious crisis and reacted sharply to it. They both also passed through a subsequent period of repentance from which Griffin was to move to a religious life, Joyce to a secular creed of his own devising. Their reactions, opposite in direction, are alike in that they are both extremes of behaviour. Joyce failed to survive as Catholic, Griffin as artist. Neither succeeded in coming to terms with his original context. Both men seriously considered becoming priests, neither persevered in this. There is even a special irony in the fact that Griffin sought eventual refuge from the world with the Christian Brothers, the teaching Order whose simple pieties the Clongownian soul of Stephen Dedalus both recognised and shrank from in that celebrated encounter on the bridge near the Bull Wall, in Chapter 4 of *A Portrait of the Artist as a Young Man*. From Rome and Trieste and Paris, Joyce pestered his Dublin relatives and friends for tit-bits of information about the city and its life and Griffin, similarly distanced from his well-springs in an unfriendly London, wrote to his brother in Ireland:

My anecdotes are all short stories, illustrative of manners and scenery precisely as they stand in the south of Ireland, never daring to travel out of perfect and easy probability. Could you not send me materials for a few short tales, laying the scene about the sea-coast – Kilkee? novelty at least. Reality you know is all the rage now.[7]

Griffin, hiding away in his 'mouse-hole' near St Paul's, unable to appear on the streets until after dark because of the tattered state of his clothing, brings to mind the Joyce who lived from hand to mouth in Paris during his first visits to that city. These two share many characteristics, many experiences. Both were proud, aloof, intensely conscious of the fragmented Irish tradition which made it so difficult for them to function serenely in their artistic roles. Almost a century divides Griffin's most famous novel, *The Collegians*, from Joyce's *Ulysses* but both are richly-peopled Irish books, great social novels which, however different in technique, have in common their richness of colour, their humour and their delight in the nuances of Anglo-Irish talk. Those two ruinously haughty creatures, Hardress Cregan and Stephen Dedalus, are cousins under the skin. Whenever the rich confusion of the Anglo-Irish tradition is meaningfully explored such figures appear in the literature, often in contrast to opposing and antithetical figures with whom they dovetail or do symbolic battle. Joyce himself has provided an entire gallery of such couples, culminating in the Shem and Shaun of *Finnegans Wake*. Griffin's Hardress Cregan and Kyrle Daly prepare us for the strange contest between the powerful shade of Michael Furey and the briefly complacent Gabriel Conroy in *The Dead*. They take us also to the sexual strife between Richard Rowan and Robert Hand in *Exiles*, that strange specimen of Ibsenised Anglo-Irish drama which reaches its climax in passionately melodramatic dialogue which might have been written for Hardress Cregan and his Eily:

BERTHA: I am yours. (*In a whisper.*) If I died this moment, I am yours.
RICHARD: (*Still gazing at her and speaking as if to an absent person.*) I have wounded my soul for you – a deep wound of doubt which can never be healed. I can never know, never in this world. I do not wish to know or to believe. I do not care. It is not in the darkness of belief that I desire you. But in restless living wounding doubt. To hold you by no bonds, even of love, to be united with

you in body and soul in utter nakedness – for this I longed. And
now I am tired for a while, Bertha. My wound tires me. (*He stretches
himself out wearily along the lounge. Bertha holds his hand, still
speaking very softly.*)
BERTHA: Forget me, Dick, Forget me and love me again as you did
the first time. I want my lover. To meet him, to go to him, to give
myself to him. You, Dick, O, my strange wild lover, come back to
me again! (*She closes her eyes.*)[8]

Again, in *Ulysses*, Stephen Dedalus and Bloom comprehensively
develop this pattern and the direction of Joyce's mature
curiosity was conveyed in his remark to Frank Budgen during
the writing of *Ulysses*: 'I have just got a letter asking me why I
don't give Bloom a rest. The writer of it wants more Stephen.
But Stephen no longer interests me to the same extent. He has
a shape that can't be changed.'[9] Joyce would seem to be indicating here that, despite the charismatic charm of the Michael
Fureys, the Hardress Cregans, the Stephen Dedaluses, it is the
Gabriel Conroys, the Kyrle Dalys and the Leopold Blooms who
survive and develop when the romantic sensitives have fallen
silent.

A great many other Irish writers apart from Joyce have
experienced the duality which Griffin explored through Hardress
Cregan and his friend, Kyrle Daly. Shaw's Larry Doyle and
Tom Broadbent, opponents and partners in that seminally
important play, *John Bull's Other Island*, come instantly to
mind. The brilliantly written exchanges between these two in
the first act of the play, exchanges which ricochet from Doyle's
passionate sentimentality to Broadbent's bluff pragmatism, from
white-hot sincerity to profound comic irony, call to mind the
exchanges between Hardress and Kyrle in Chapter 13 of *The
Collegians*, staid though the latter may be in comparison with
the Shavian high jinks. The styles may differ but the ingredients
of the discussions are the same. More recently, the sensitive hero
with a nervous dread of polite society has been developed by
Samuel Beckett into his seedy solipsist, Murphy, who shuns the
world and, after a brief and unsatisfactory surrender to desire,
finally destroys himself in a moment of black comic melodrama.
Flann O'Brien, with many a sardonic glance at Stephen Dedalus,
revives the type in the nameless hero of *At-Swim-Two-Birds*
and provides him with the acquiescent Brinsley as his com-

panion and audience. The figure reappears in the sombre fiction of John McGahern in the form of young Mahoney of *The Dark*, and in the realms of comedy one recalls Patrick Kavanagh's Tarry Flynn counterpointed against his cannier companion, Eusebius Cassidy. Perhaps even Synge's Christy Mahon, astounded over 'two fine women fighting for the likes of me' is not altogether unrelated to the braggadocio Hardress who undergoes his own troubles with a brace of females, though with noticeably less comic results.

The further one extends the exploration the more one realises that in his best-known novel Gerald Griffin was exploring themes which are central to the Anglo-Irish tradition. It would do but poor service to a vast body of fine works to offer any unduly facile interpretation of the recurring involvement of the literature with such contrasts and oppositions, but we may hazard the suggestion that as they reappear these companions, opponents, friends, rivals reflect something of importance in the national character and the developing public scene. Without imposing unduly precise identifications which would only distort or impoverish particular works, we may allow our imaginations to deploy contrasts between romanticism and realism, between intransigence and adaptability, between defiance and compromise, between a dead but still powerful past and an unsatisfactory but unavoidable present. These variously imagined *personae* are no less than the rotating chairmen of the continuing debate between modern Ireland and its Gaelic past. The exchanges run the gamut from abuse to satire, from invective to geniality, and perhaps express themselves most characteristically in richly sardonic comedy. Yeats, compelled to revaluation when he saw Paudeen transformed into Cuchulain, enshrined these productive oppositions by responding to an historical moment with the imaginative generosity which transcends history's necessarily blunter verdicts:

> Hearts with one purpose alone
> Through summer and winter seem
> Enchanted to a stone
> To trouble the living stream.
> The horse that comes from the road,
> The rider, the birds that range

From cloud to tumbling cloud,
Minute by minute they change;
A shadow of cloud on the stream
Changes minute by minute;
A horse-hoof slides on the brim,
And a horse plashes within it;
The long-legged moor-hens dive,
And hens to moor-cocks call;
Minute by minute they live;
The stone's in the midst of all.

Too long a sacrifice
Can make a stone of the heart.
O when may it suffice?
That is Heaven's part, our part
To murmur name upon name,
As a mother names her child
When sleep at last has come
On limbs that had run wild.[10]

Many Irish writers begin as regional writers and subsequently strive to reach a wider, more cosmopolitan audience. Ordinarily, the line of development is away from regionalism to some kind of fictional mainstream. In our own day, Edna O'Brien and Brian Moore are notable examples of this tendency. The former abandoned her Irish themes after a time and wrote a purposefully non-Irish novel, *Casualties of Peace*. In works such as *I Am Mary Dunne* and *The Great Victorian Collection* Moore seems a long way from the Belfast of Judith Hearne. In the nineteenth century Charles Lever is an example of an ambitious novelist who deliberately, though without much success, made a move from Dublin to London at the time of the composition of *The Knight of Gwynne*. Griffin, in his career, reversed the process. The failure of his dramatic ambitions, his disgust with the shifts and posturings of his protean journalistic endeavours and the contemporary vogue for the regional novel drove him back to his native country in a desperate search for his identity. In discovering his literary destiny he discovered his own people and found them broken and despairing, uneducated, exploited, wretched and desperately poor. The more he came to know his unhappy fellow-countrymen, the more his metropolitan dreams of fame faded into the background.

One important respect in which he differs from Joyce is in

his lack of a formal education. It was a deficiency which troubled him throughout his life. He tried to remedy the situation belatedly by attending lectures at London University and he may, in this connection, have instinctively understood his own predicament. For one result of his unsatisfactory schooling was that he never built around his considerable talent any protective intellectual carapace. He is ever a creature of impulse, full of 'nature', quick to take offence, generous to a fault, forever turning an unprotected sensibility to the barbs of a cruel world. He found it possible to make friends but difficult not to bicker with them over trivialities. In this respect his troubled relationship with John Banim is the saddest example of his dangerous touchiness. Only with his own family and sometimes with the Fishers does he seem to have felt the confidence of total commitment. The tragedy was that he imported exactly the same simplicities into his work. When Daniel tried to rally him into a happy surrender to his genuine creative impulses he was met by a desperate and angry assertion of the impossibility of a writer's retaining his personal independence of the creatures of his fancy:

He complained on one occasion of his inability to manage some particular scene. I recommended him to pay no attention to those scruples but to follow the bent of his natural feeling, and fling himself fully into the subject. 'Oh, but,' he said, 'that is the difficulty: I don't think one is justified in putting himself into the condition that it requires.' I could hardly understand his meaning for some time, and began to make very light of such a notion, until he lost all patience, and said with vehemence, 'Oh, but you do not know, you cannot know, the state an author puts himself into in working out such scenes: how can it be right of him to put himself in the position of each particular character, and endeavour to kindle in his own breast all the passions of that character even for the moment?'[11]

This tortured outburst proves both that Griffin was a born novelist and that he could not hope to survive as one. Such desperately intense involvement bespeaks both great creative drive and a ruinous battle between the writer's morality and his aesthetic.

François Mauriac has written with compassionate perception about this very dilemma with which he as a Catholic novelist was also familiar. What he has to say is so germane to Griffin's predicament that it seems worth quoting at some length. Mauriac first outlines two extreme points of view, one which insists on the absolute independence of the artist and the other demanding that the novelist 'must write with fear and trembling under the eye of the Trinity'. He comments:

Then, between these two opposing camps, there is the huge crowd of novelists who fluctuate and hesitate. On the one hand they admit that their work is valuable only inasmuch as it apprehends living men in their completeness, in their heights and in their depths – the human creature as he is. They feel that any intervention in the unfolding of their characters – even to prove the truth of what they believe – is an abuse. They feel a sincere revulsion against falsifying life. On the other hand, they know that they are treading on dangerous ground, and that their intense desire to depict human emotions and passions may have an incalculable and permanent effect on the lives of many people. Every novelist worthy of the name and every playwright who is a born Christian suffers from the torment of this dilemma.[12]

In spite of the torment of this dilemma, Griffin achieved much between the publication of *Holland-Tide* in 1827 and his withdrawal from the world a decade later. In that time he displayed in his best work 'the most alert eye which had yet looked upon the Irish scene'.[13] He showed himself to be one of the most convincing users of the regional English of the province of Munster, peopling his pages with hosts of richly-spoken and memorable figures, using the emergent English of the Irish poor for all kinds of effects, both humorous and tragic. At his best he is a powerfully realistic depictor of the troubled Ireland of his time. The ragged Irish scarecrows who crowd his pages prepare us for the horrors which fell upon the country in the dreadful decade after Griffin's early death. His discerning account of their irresponsible overlords is equally accurate and prophetic. In novels such as *The Collegians* and *Tracy's Ambition* we find vividly recorded the dark Ireland which lies between the Union and the Great Famine. If a writer deserves to be judged on his best work, then Griffin may safely be accounted one of the great Irish realistic writers. When one turns to analysing the causes of his artistic decline one finds that he eventually succumbed to temptations which have visited even the greatest writers. Yeats might almost have had him in mind when he wrote:

The intellect of man is forced to choose
Perfection of the life, or of the work,
And if he take the second must refuse
A heavenly mansion, raging in the dark.

When all that story's finished, what's the news?
In luck or out the toil has left its mark:
That old perplexity an empty purse,
Or the day's vanity, the night's remorse.[14]

If Gerald Griffin ultimately lacked the stark determination required for 'raging in the dark' and opted for perfection of the life rather than of the work, he would be a harsh critic, and no Irishman, who would fail to grant that he achieved as much as his strange nature and terrible times permitted.

Appendix

Adventures of an Irish Giant

One of the more curious and intriguing Griffin survivals, the exact history of which it is now difficult to trace, is a full-length novel entitled *Adventures of an Irish Giant,* first published as a novel in Boston some dozen or so years after its author's death. This work is not mentioned in Michael Sadleir's extensive and detailed account of the works of Griffin in *XIX-Century Fiction,* nor does Daniel mention it in the *Life.* The first reference to it which can be traced is in a letter which Charles Dickens addressed to Griffin from 48 Doughty Street, London on January 29, 1838:

Sir,

Mr Bentley has handed to me the first part of your 'Adventures of an Irish Giant'. As the subscribers to the *Miscellany* have complained bitterly of our numerous continuations, we have been obliged to discontinue them.[1]

This letter seems to have come eventually into the possession of a Mr James Hayes of Ennis, County Clare, who, in a brief note in *The Bookworm* in 1892, describes the letter and how it finally reached Griffin at his brother's home at 62 George Street, Limerick. Hayes then goes on to speculate about the fate of the manuscript referred to by Dickens:

But what became of the 'First Part' of our friend of the 'Irish Giant', so summarily dismissed from the *Miscellany* in favour of 'Complete Papers each of which could be begun and completed in the same Number?' I believe he never found his way back to Ireland or Boston, U.S., but slept in a pigeon-hole in Bentley's; and when he awoke, if he ever did awake, his creator was sleeping the sleep of the just. In 1851–52 'The Adventures of an Irish Giant', in twenty-six chapters, appeared in serial form in *Duffy's Fireside Magazine,* a work now become scarce. About the same time, in agreement with Mr Duffy, Mr P. Donoghue, of Boston, U.S. published the same matter – tradi-

tion in Mr Duffy's office says *more*. My impression is that Gerald
Griffin did not begin a second part after the rejection of the First – a
purely accidental rejection and not on its merits – as the author's
'valuable assistance' was still sought – and that the copy for what was
published consisted of his first rough draft polished and connected
by another hand. I make this assertion from internal evidence alone,
and I do not know with any certainty what fraction of the 'Irish
Giant' appeared in America. What I have read in the *Fireside Magazine* certainly displayed the power and isolated beauties of the
master hand, but the strong electric current which should flow
uninterruptedly through the 'Irish Giant' is often weakened by
'breaks' and imperfect 'conductors'.[2]

Precisely how Duffy acquired the manuscript of *Adventures
of an Irish Giant* is not clear. Sadleir indicates that Duffy
acquired the plates and type of the second issue of the collected
edition of the *Life and Works of Gerald Griffin* in the middle
1840s. The manuscript may have come his way at this time,
though there is no obvious direct connection here, since *Adventures of an Irish Giant* formed no part of the collected *Works*.
The date of its composition is equally a matter of speculation.
It is not known when Griffin submitted it to Bentley or how long
Bentley retained it before giving it to Dickens. Even the date of
the Boston publication of the work in novel form is not easy to
establish exactly. The copy of the work inspected by the present
writer is in the Joly Collection in the National Library of
Ireland. Its title page describes the work as 'by the late Gerald
Griffin'. The publisher is named as Patrick Donahoe, 25 Franklin
Street, Boston. Donahoe (1811–1901), an eminent and wealthy
Irish-American, was owner and editor of the Boston *Pilot* and
publisher for various Irish-American writers of note. Entries
in the Boston city directories do not show him as having had
an address at 25 Franklin Street but he is found at 3 Franklin
Street from 1852 to 53 and at 23 Franklin Street from 1854 to
67. The second of these addresses is close enough to 25 Franklin
Street to suggest that publication of the novel may have taken
place about 1854. No entry for *Adventures of an Irish Giant* is to
be found in the Catalog of the Library of Congress or in the
National Union Catalog.[3]

The 'tradition in Mr Duffy's office' to which James Hayes
refers, suggesting that Donahoe had added to the text, is an

erroneous one. Comparison of the text in *Duffy's Fireside Magazine*, 1850–52, with the text of Donahoe's Boston volume shows the two to be identical apart from a sizeable number of minor errors in the American version, due presumably to careless proof-reading. Hayes's suggestion that the copy for what was published by Duffy may have consisted of Griffin's 'first rough draft polished and connected by another hand' could have some substance in it, particularly if we assume that the novel is a late rather than an early Griffin work. The novel begins strongly but loses much of its early drive fairly soon, with realism quickly giving way to melodrama. This may be what Hayes has in mind when he writes of 'breaks' and 'imperfect conductors'. The book is, in any case, of considerable interest to the student of Griffin's work. The opening chapters are in his best vein, combining genuinely humorous depiction of Irish rural life with potent satirical condemnation of the landlords and squireens who so vilely exploited the people of Griffin's Ireland. The mood and flavour of this part of the book are sometimes reminiscent of Griffin's short novel, *The Rivals* (1829) and sometimes of parts of *The Collegians* (1829).

At the beginning we are introduced to the miserable village of Ballymahon, a wretched hole so poor that the priest, the doctor and the Protestant curate were 'almost the only three individuals in the place from whose habits it could be demonstrated that the human species belonged to animals of the carnivorous kind'. We meet two dispensary doctors. Griffin, with two M.D.s in his immediate family, is generally good on doctors and country dispensaries. Dr Vanderkyst is an hilarious horror, a drunken roistering lout who cares more for hunting and carousing than for his peasant patients. Dr O'Gorman, on the other hand, is a dedicated medical man whose only fault is that he tends to let his interest in the disease take precedence over his interest in the patient:

A lovely young mother dying in the arms of a distracted husband and weeping children, was spoken of by him as 'a very interesting case of hyperemia' and a dissipated tradesman snatched suddenly from the bosom of a helpless family, figured, in the doctor's memoranda, one of the 'most beautiful internal lesions in the world'. (p. 27)

Vanderkyst is called to deliver a child, Patcheen Goggin, the Giant of the novel's title and sets off drunkenly to perform a quite unnecessary operation:

When Martin returned to the room, he was startled at seeing his master with the huge knives in his hand, examining and comparing the edges of each in turn, one with another, and finding at the same time some little difficulty in keeping his erect position. Having satisfied himself as to the eligibility of the instruments, he vouchsafed as well as a slight defect of utterance, partly occasioned by habitual impetuosity of temperament, and partly by the indulgences of the evening, would allow him, to intimate something of his intentions to the bewildered Martin.

'Martin,' said he with emphasis, as he slightly brandished one of the knives in his hand, 'th – this is a ca – ca – case – hic – for the – hico – caesarean operation.'

Martin had never heard of this operation, so he could hardly be expected to know much about it. However knowing what was the matter with the woman, and seeing the huge knives, and combining both ideas, he was enabled to form a correct idea of the nature of the proceeding contemplated by his master. As his natural feeling of humanity preponderated in some slight degree over his confidence in the skill of Dr Vanderkyst, more especially in his present condition, some notion may be formed of the horror with which the conjecture was accompanied. (pp. 17–18)

Fortunately, Patcheen Goggin's mother manages to produce her child without Dr Vanderkyst's assistance. The child grows to an unusual height and the parents despair of finding him a suitable occupation. His father, a carpenter by trade, canvasses the possibilities:

'I don't know from Adam what I'll do with him,' he said to his wife, in a tone of deep perplexity – 'he's more like a *gad* or a fishing-rod than anything else.'

'And 'tisn't that same,' rejoiced Mrs Coggin, 'only all he aits. You might as well be throwin' praties down the well of Knock Fierna, that they says has no bottom at all to it. There's no fillin' him. Where he puts his diet is like a Connemara stockin', the more that's put in it, the more it sthretches.'

'Thrue for you; an' it isn't learnin' to do with less he'll be,' replied her husband.

'Couldn't you make a tailor of him, Dinny, achree, an' have done with him?'

'Arra howl woman, what tailor? What 'ud he do with his legs? Sure if he crossed 'em they'd cover the floore.'

'Or a shoemaker itself?'

'Nonsense! he should have a stool as tall as a horse.' (pp. 24-5)

The parents finally hit upon the plan of exhibiting their un-
naturally lengthy offspring in a box as a sort of circus curiosity.
Patcheen Goggin learns of their intention and runs away from
home. At this point the novel deteriorates from the level of
realism where Griffin was at his comic best to that of improbably
melodramatic contrivance where he was often at his worst. We
lose sight of the Irish Giant altogether and embark on an
unconvincing story about a beautiful orphan girl and the
mysteries surrounding her birth. The background of grasping
squireens and landlords preying on a helpless peasantry is well
maintained throughout but the plot gradually becomes impos-
sibly contrived. This part of the book is either very bad Griffin
or else, as Hayes suggests, the scissors-and-paste work of another
hand.

If, at the beginning of 1838, when Dickens wrote to him,
Griffin had not completed more than a first instalment of the
novel, it seems unlikely that he then completed the work
himself. By that time his thoughts were already turning steadily
towards the religious life. The last weeks of April and the
beginning of May found him undertaking a tour of Scotland
with his brother, Daniel. In August he informed his family of
his intention of becoming a Christian Brother. He would seem
to have had neither the time nor the inclination for serious novel
writing at this point in his career. There is also, of course, the
possibility that the work is from an earlier date and that
Bentley had held the first instalment for some time before
sending it to Dickens, but there is no such suggestion in Dickens's
letter.

Notes

1. THE PERIOD, FAMILY BACKGROUND AND EARLY LIFE

1 Edmund Curtis, *A History of Ireland* (London, 1936) and Denis Gwynn, *The Struggle for Catholic Emancipation, 1750–1829* (London, 1928) have been drawn upon for information about the historical background of the period.
2 Quoted by Gwynn, *Struggle for Catholic Emancipation*, 1.
3 Ibid. 8.
4 Ibid. 14.
5 Daniel Griffin, *Life of Gerald Griffin Esq.*, 2nd edn (Dublin, 1857), 148–9. (See Textual Note.)
6 Ibid. 189–90.
7 *The Collegians* (London, 1829), I, 184. (See Textual Note.)
8 *Life*, 380–1.
9 Ethel Mannin, *Two Studies in Integrity* (London, 1954), 102–3.
10 *Life*, 314.
11 Daniel Griffin, *Life of Gerald Griffin Esq.* (London, 1843), 7–8. (See Textual Note.)
12 M. Moloney, 'Limerick and Gerald Griffin', *North Munster Antiquarian Journal*, II, i (Spring 1940), 4–11.
13 *Life*, 32.
14 *The Rivals and Tracy's Ambition* (London, 1829), I, 146–53.
15 P. J. Dowling, *The Hedge Schools of Ireland*, rev. edn. (Cork, 1968), 25.
16 *Life*, 227.
17 Ibid. 33.
18 *Lit. Gaz.* 389 (July 3, 1824), 429.
19 *Life*, 55–6.
20 See Appendix.
21 *Life*, 62.

2. THE LONDON PERIOD: 1823–1827

1 *Life*, 79.
2 Ibid. 94.
3 *Blackwood's*, XVII, ci (June 1825), 727–31.
4 *Citizen*, II, x (Aug. 1840), 158–64.
5 *Nation*, I, 9 (Dec. 10, 1842), 140.

6 *Life*, 78.
7 Ibid. 85–6. 8 Ibid. 115.
9 Ibid. 110. 10 Ibid. 123.
11 The series began in *Lit. Gaz.* 385 (June 5, 1824), 361 and ended in *Lit. Gaz.* 404 (Oct. 16, 1824), 669–70.
12 *Lit. Gaz.* 397 (Aug. 28, 1824), 555.
13 *Lit. Gaz.* 400 (Sept. 18, 1824), 606.
14 *Life*, 117–18. 15 Ibid. 122.
16 Ibid. 151. 17 Ibid. 128.
18 Ibid. 19 Ibid. 127–8.
20 Ibid. 127. 21 Ibid. 216.
22 *NLF*, iii, 59 (July 1825), 50.
23 *NLF*, iii, 64 (Aug. 1825), 136–7.
24 *Life*, 164. 25 Ibid. 165.
26 Ibid. 164. 27 *NLF*, iii, 72 (Oct. 1825), 257.
28 *NLF*, iii, 77 (Nov. 1825), 342. 29 *Life*, 142.
30 Ibid. 187. 31 Ibid. 154–5.
32 Ibid. 33 Ibid. 170.

3. EARLY PROSE WORKS

1 Padraic Colum, Introduction to *The Collegians* (Dublin 1918), xv.
2 *Holland-Tide* (London, 1827), 208.
3 Ibid. 25–6.
4 E. Œ. Somerville, 'Stage Irishmen and Others', *Strayaways* (London, 1920), 248.
5 Donald Davie, 'Gerald Griffin's "The Collegians"', *The Dublin Magazine*, n.s. xxviii, 2 (April–June 1953), 28.
6 *Holland-Tide*, 195–7.
7 Thomas Flanagan, *The Irish Novelists 1800–1850* (New York, 1959), 216.
8 *The Journal of Sir Walter Scott*, ed. W. E. K. Anderson (Oxford, 1972), 444.
9 *Tales of the Munster Festivals* (London, 1827), i, xvi.
10 Ibid. i, xvii.
11 Ibid. i, xviii.
12 Ibid. i, xix–xx.
13 See Griffin's two letters, *Life*, 148–9 and 189–90, cited ch. 1, notes 5 and 6.
14 *Tales of the Munster Festivals*, i, xx.
15 Ibid. i, xxii.
16 Ibid. i, 8.
17 *Life*, 224.
18 *Tales of the Munster Festivals* (London, 1842), 246–7.
19 *Tales of the Munster Festivals*, i, 25.
20 Ibid. i, 283–4.

21 Ibid. ɪ, 311–12.
23 Ibid. ɪ, 291–2.
25 Ibid. ɪ, 350–1.

22 Ibid. ɪ, 238.
24 Ibid. ɪ, 201–3.
26 Ibid. ɪɪ, 78–9.

4. 'THE COLLEGIANS'

1 *Life*, 198–9.
2 Ibid. 223. (The 'first series' referred to here is *Tales of the Munster Festivals*. The 'second series' is *The Collegians*.)
3 Ibid. 224.
4 A convenient summary of the affair will be found in 'Footsteps of the Colleen Bawn' by T. E. Galt-Gamble, *New Ireland Review*, vɪ (Sept. 1896), 27–38. A more recent account, incorporating an adaptation of *The Collegians*, is *Death Sails the Shannon* by W. MacLysaght and Sigerson Clifford (Tralee, 1953).

5 *Life*, 206–7.
6 Flanagan, *Irish Novelists*, 220.
7 *The Collegians*, ɪ, 6–7.
8 Ibid. ɪ, 85–6.
9 Flanagan, *Irish Novelists*, 223.
10 *The Collegians*, ɪ, 170.
11 Ibid, ɪ, 210–11.
12 Ibid. ɪɪɪ, 173–4.
13 Ibid. ɪɪɪ, 179–80.
14 Ibid. ɪɪɪ, 187–8.
15 Ibid. ɪɪɪ, 189–91.
16 Flanagan, *Irish Novelists*, 230.
17 *Life*, 187.
18 *The Collegians*, ɪ, 53–4.
19 Ibid. ɪ, 248.
20 Ibid, ɪ, 274–5.
21 Ibid. ɪ, 278–9.
22 Ibid. ɪ, 279.
23 Ibid. ɪ, 280–1.
24 Ibid. ɪ, 282.
25 Ibid. ɪ, 329–30.
26 Ibid. ɪɪ, 100–1.
27 Colum, Introduction to *The Collegians* (Dublin, 1918), xi.
28 Hero of Thornton Wilder's novel, *Heaven's My Destination* (1934).
29 *Life*, 99.
30 Ibid. 175–93.
31 *Tales of the Munster Festivals*, Sig. I 3r.
32 *Life*, 170.
33 Ibid. 225.

5. REGIONAL WRITER, HISTORIAN, MORALIST, LOVER

1 *The Rivals and Tracy's Ambition*, ɪ, 146–53.
2 Ibid. ɪ, 36–7.
3 Ibid. ɪ, 81–2.
4 Flanagan, *Irish Novelists*, 242.
5 *The Rivals and Tracy's Ambition*, ɪ, 59–60.
6 Ibid. ɪɪ, 37.
7 Ibid. ɪɪ, 40–1.
8 Ibid. ɪɪ, 111–12.
9 Ibid. ɪɪ, 131–2.
10 Ibid. ɪɪ, 276.
11 Ibid. ɪɪɪ, 292.
12 Ibid. ɪɪ, 188–9.
13 Ibid. ɪɪ, 206–7.
14 Ibid. ɪɪɪ, 296.
15 Ibid. ɪɪɪ, 297–8.

16 Ibid. III, 299.   17 Ibid. III, 300–1.
18 *Life*, 271–2.   19 Ibid. 276–7.
20 *The Christian Physiologist* (London, 1830), x.
21 Ibid. xi–xii.
22 *Life*, 277.   23 *The Christian Physiologist*, 375.
24 *Life*, 381.   25 Ibid. 231.
26 Ibid. 235.   27 Ibid. 286.
28 Flanagan, *Irish Novelists*, 235. 29 *Life*, 239.
30 *Journal of Sir Walter Scott*, ed. Anderson, 444.
31 *Life and Letters of Maria Edgeworth*, ed. A. J. C. Hare (2 vols.,
   London, 1894), II, 167.
32 *Life*, 238.
33 Ibid. 238–9.   34 *Lit. Gaz.* 781 (Jan. 7, 1832), 4–5.
35 *Life*, 216.   36 Ibid. 272–3.
37 Ibid. 383.   38 Ibid. 248.
39 Ibid. 245.   40 Ibid. 246–7.
41 Ibid. 248.   42 Ibid. 249.
43 Ibid. 251.   44 Ibid. 253.
45 Ibid. 257–8.   46 Ibid. 261.
47 John Cronin, 'Some Unpublished Letters of Gerald Griffin',
   Eire-Ireland, IX, iv (Winter 1974), 46.
48 *Life*, 296.
49 Cronin, *Eire-Ireland*, IX, iv, 63–4.
50 *Life*, 315.
51 Ibid. 319.   52 Ibid. 322–3.
53 Ibid. 396–7.   54 Ibid. 372–3.

6. THE LAST PHASE

1 *Life*, 307.
2 Ibid. 311–14.
3 For an account of the affair see L. A. G. Strong, *The Minstrel Boy:
   A Portrait of Tom Moore* (London, 1937), 206–11. *The Letters of
   Thomas Moore*, ed. W. S. Dowden (2 vols., Oxford, 1964), II,
   750–1 and 757–61 also provide helpful detail.
4 *Memoirs, Journal and Correspondence of Thomas Moore*, ed. Lord
   John Russell (8 vols., London, 1853–6), VI, 305–6.
5 Ibid. 301–2.   6 *Life*, 309–10.
7 Ibid. 310.   8 Ibid. 310.
9 Ibid. 311.   10 Ibid. 313.
11 Somerville, 'Stage Irishmen and Others', *Strayaways*, 248–50.
12 *Tales of My Neighbourhood* (London, 1835), I, 288.
13 Ibid. II, 181–2.
14 Ibid. II, 303.   15 Ibid. III, 307–8.
16 *Life*, 324.   17 Ibid. 149.
18 Ibid. 324–5.   19 Ibid. 326ff.

20 For the text of this letter see Cronin, *Eire-Ireland*, IX, iv, 48–9.
21 *Life*, 330–64.   22 Ibid. 365.
23 Ibid. 382.   24 Cronin, *Eire-Ireland*, IX, iv, 55.
25 *Life*, 383.   26 Cronin, *Eire-Ireland*, IX, iv, 59.
27 Ibid. 60.   28 *Life*, 385.
29 Cronin, *Eire-Ireland*, IX, iv, 60–1.

7. POSTHUMOUS PUBLICATIONS AND GRIFFIN'S LITERARY SIGNIFICANCE

1 Michael Sadleir, *XIX-Century Fiction* (London, 1951), I, 157.
2 *Life*, 171–2.
3 Ibid. 372.
4 *Macready's Reminiscences and Selections from his Diaries and Letters*, ed. Sir Frederick Pollock (London, 1876), 515.
5 Ibid. 519–20.
6 *Life*, 98–9.
7 Ibid. 154–5.
8 James Joyce, *Exiles* (London, 1918), 158.
9 Frank Budgen, *James Joyce and the Making of 'Ulysses'* (Oxford, 1972), 107.
10 W. B. Yeats, *Collected Poems* (London, 1952), 204.
11 *Life*, 270–1.
12 François Mauriac, *God and Mammon*, ch. 5 (quoted in *Novelists on the Novel*, ed. Miriam Allott (London, 1959), 106).
13 Flanagan, *Irish Novelists*, 216.
14 Yeats, *Collected Poems*, 278–9.

APPENDIX

1 *The Letters of Charles Dickens*, I, ed. Madeline House and Graham Storey (Oxford, 1965), 364.
2 James Hayes, 'Adventures of an Irish Giant', *The Bookworm*, V, 41 (1892), 6–7.
3 The assistance of Mrs Gail F. Borden, Reference Department, Library of the Boston Athenaeum and of Mr John Alden, Keeper of Rare Books, Boston Public Library, is gratefully acknowledged. According to Mr Alden, *Adventures of an Irish Giant* does not appear in Donahoe's catalogue of books available in 1869.

Bibliography

BIBLIOGRAPHIES

Bateson, F. W. (ed.), *Cambridge Bibliography of English Literature*, Cambridge, 1940–57, III, p. 485.

Leclaire, Lucien, *A General Analytical Bibliography of the Regional Novelists of the British Isles, 1800–1950*, Clermont-Ferrand, 1954, pp. 54–5.

Sadleir, Michael, *XIX-Century Fiction*, London, 1951, I, pp. 155–9.

Watson, George (ed.), *The New Cambridge Bibliography of English Literature*, III, Cambridge, 1969, pp. 931–2.

MAJOR WORKS BY GERALD GRIFFIN: EARLY EDITIONS

Holland-Tide, London, 1827.

Tales of the Munster Festivals, 3 vols., London, 1827.

The Dilemma of Phadrig, London, 1828 (*The Literary Souvenir*, pp. 3–19).

The Collegians, 3 vols., London, 1829.

The Rivals and Tracy's Ambition, 3 vols., London, 1829.

The Christian Physiologist, London, 1830.

The Invasion, 4 vols., London, 1832.

Tales of My Neighbourhood, 3 vols., London, 1835.

The Bishop's Island, London, 1835 (*The Literary Souvenir*, pp. 52–6).

The Duke of Monmouth, 3 vols., London, 1836.

Talis Qualis or Tales of the Jury Room, 3 vols., London, 1842.

Gisippus, London, 1842.

Life and Works of Gerald Griffin, 8 vols., London, 1842–3.

    Vol. I. Daniel Griffin, *Life of Gerald Griffin Esq.*, London, 1843.

    Vol. II. *The Collegians*, London, 1842.

    Vol. III. *Tales of the Munster Festivals*, London, 1842.

    Vol. IV. *The Rivals and Tracy's Ambition*, London, 1842.

    Vol. V. *Holland-Tide*, London, 1842.

    Vol. VI. *The Duke of Monmouth*, London, 1842.

    Vol. VII. *Talis Qualis or Tales of the Jury Room*, London, 1842.

    Vol. VIII. *The Poetical Works*, London, 1843.

Adventures of an Irish Giant, Boston [1854?].
Reasons For My Faith, Dublin, 1878 (*Irish Monthly*, VI, 148–57).
The Holy Island, Dublin, 1878 (*Irish Monthly*, VI, 566–72 and 611–20).

TRANSLATION

Die Schulfreunde, trans. Karl von Killinger, 2 vols., Stuttgart and
Tübingen, 1843.

ARTICLES, POEMS AND REVIEWS BY GERALD GRIFFIN

'My Soul is Sick and Lone', *Lit. Gaz.* 389 (July 3, 1824), 428–9.

Horae Monomienses
    'Irish Satire', *Lit. Gaz.* 385 (June 5, 1824), 361.
    'Letter II – The Irish Funeral Cry', *Lit. Gaz.* 387 (June 19, 1824),
        392–3.
    'Letter III – St Sinon's Isle', *Lit. Gaz.* 388 (June 26, 1824), 408.
    'Letter IV – The Bells of St Mary's', *Lit. Gaz.* 393 (July 31, 1824),
        490–1.
    'Irish Satire – Letter V. *The Dispensary – Village Literature*', *Lit.
        Gaz.* 397 (Aug. 28, 1824), 554–5.
    'Horae Monomienses – Letter VI, *Local Superstitions*', *Lit. Gaz.* 399
        (Sept. 11, 1824), 586.
    'Horae Monomienses – Letter VII', *Lit. Gaz.* 400 (Sept 18, 1824),
        605–6.
    'Horae Monominenses – Letter VIII', *Lit. Gaz.* 402 (Oct. 2, 1824),
        637–8.
    'Horae Monominenses – Letter IX, *Rockites*', *Lit. Gaz.* 404 (Oct. 16,
        1824), 669–70.

Sketches of Manners: Professed People
    'No. 1 – Authors', *NLF*, II, 37 (Feb. 19, 1825), 116.
    'No. 2 – Punsters', *NLF*, II, 38 (Feb. 26, 1825), 132–3.
    'No. III – Painters', *NLF*, II, 39 (March 5, 1825), 149–50.
    'No. IV – Musicians', *NLF*, II, 40 (March 12, 1825), 167.
    'No. V – Actors', *NLF*, II, 41 (March 19, 1825), 182–3.
    'No. VI – Political Economists', *NLF*, II, 44 (April 9, 1825), 229.
'Epistle to Mr Liston On His Return To London', *NLF*, II, 55 (June
    25, 1825), 404–5.
'Hints For The Formation Of A New Musical Entertainment', *NLF*,
    III, 59 (July 23, 1825), 49–50.
'Faults Of The New Operatic Experiment', *NLF*, III, 64 (Aug. 27,
    1825), 136–7.
'Sheridan And His Biographer', *NLF*, III, 72 (Oct. 22, 1825), 257–8.
Mary-le-Bone Lyrics
    'I. To the Little Blackamoor at the Haymarket', *NLF*, III, 66 (Sept.
        10, 1825), 165–6.

'II. *Mr Graham to Miss Dawson in the Clouds*', *NLF*, III, 67 (Sept. 17, 1825), 184–5.

'III. *To the Flying American*', *NLF*, III, 70 (Oct. 8, 1825), 230–1.

'IV. *To Claude Seurat, on leaving London*', *NLF*, III, 71 (Oct. 15, 1825), 246.

'V. *Recipe for the Belle Ideale*', *NLF*, III, 72 (Oct. 22, 1825), 264.

'VI. *Recipe for the Beau Ideal*', *NLF*, III, 73 (Oct. 29, 1825), 279.

'VII. *To the "Nigger" Roscius*', *NLF*, III, 74 (Nov. 5, 1825), 293–4.

'VIII. *To M. Mazurier – the C.G. Jocko*', *NLF*, III, 75 (Nov. 12, 1825), 309.

ARTICLES, POEMS AND REVIEWS PROBABLY BY
GERALD GRIFFIN

'A Bird's-Eye View In The South-West Of Ireland', *Lit. Chron.* 268 (July 3, 1824), 427–8.

'A Soirée In Hades – William Shakespeare At Bow Street', *Lit. Chron.* 269 (July 10, 1824), 444–5.

'My First Play', *NLF*, II, 49 (May 14, 1825), 310–11.

'Here And There. No. VI – *Redmond Barry: My Lord Tom-and-Jerry*', *NLF*, II, 55 (June 25, 1825), 402–4.

'The Late Mr J. B. Clarke', *NLF*, II, 55 (June 25, 1825), 405.

'A Letter To Charles Kemble, Esq. And R. W. Elliston, Esq. On The Present State Of The Stage', *Blackwood's*, XVII, ci (June 1825), 727–31.

'Irish Feelings On The Loss Of Sir Francis Burdett's Bill', *NLF*, III, 59. (July 23, 1825), 58–9.

'English Drama. *Playhouse Novelties*', *NLF*, III, 60 (July 30, 1825), 73–4.

'London Visits. *Visit 50*. The King's Theatre And Velluti', *NLF*, III, 61 (Aug. 6, 1825), 84–5.

'Confessions Of A Young Author. No. 1. – *Editors and Booksellers*, and Valedictory Stanzas To Signor Velluti', *NLF*, III, 62 (Aug. 13, 1825), 102–3.

'English Opera-House. *The Tarrare – The New Singers*', *NLF*, III, 63 (Aug. 20, 1825), 121–2.

'New Nonsense Of The Political Economists', *NLF*, III, 68 (Sept. 24, 1825), 194–5.

'A Dithyrambic Ode To Monsieur Gouffe, *On his intended departure for Edinburgh*', *NLF*, III, 68 (Sept. 24, 1825), 198.

'Considerations On The Literary Joint-Stock Company; *And a New Project for the Advancement of Literature*', *NLF*, III, 68 (Sept. 24, 1825), 198–9.

'Opening Of The Winter Theatres. – The New Tragedian', *NLF*, III, 69 (Oct. 1, 1825), 218–19.

'The Theatres', *NLF*, III, 70 (Oct. 8, 1825), 231–2.

'The Traveller And The Legislator; Or, Dialogue And Dialect', *NLF*, III, 72 (Oct. 22, 1825), 264–5.

'Captain Parry', *NLF*, III, 72 (Oct. 22, 1825), 265.

'English Drama', *NLF*, III, 72 (Oct. 22, 1825), 265–6.

'To The Haytian Colonists, On The Projected French Loan', *NLF*, III, 73 (Oct. 29, 1825), 278–9.

'English Drama', *NLF*, III, 73 (Oct. 29, 1825), 279–80.

'The Day of Vengeance', *NLF*, III, 74 (Nov. 5, 1825), 291.

'The Stage-Coach Physiognomist. – No. 1', *NLF*, III, 74 (Nov. 5, 1825), 292–3.

'To Miss F. H. Kelly, *On NOT being drowned on board the Comet*', *NLF*, III, 74 (Nov. 5, 1825), 294.

'English Drama', *NLF*, III, 74 (Nov. 5, 1825), 294–5.

'The Stage-Coach Physiognomist. No. 2', *NLF*, III, 75 (Nov. 12, 1825), 308–9.

'Inhumanity of Petty Officers', *NLF*, III, 76 (Nov. 19, 1825), 324.

'The Stage-Coach Physiognomist. No. 3', *NLF*, III, 76 (Nov. 19, 1825), 325.

'English Drama', *NLF*, III, 76 (Nov. 19, 1825), 327–8.

'Mendicant Authors', *NLF*, III, 82 (Dec. 31, 1825), 419–20.

WORKS ON GERALD GRIFFIN
(in chronological order)

'Death of Gerald Griffin', *The Citizen*, II, ix (July 1840), 145–8.

'Memoir of the late Gerald Griffin', *The Citizen*, II, x (Aug. 1840), 158–64.

'National Gallery, No. II: Gerald Griffin Esq.', *The Nation*, I, 9 (Dec. 10, 1842), 140.

'Gerald Griffin', *The Nation*, I, 10 (Dec. 17, 1842), 154.

Review of *Life of Gerald Griffin Esq.*, *by his Brother*, *The Dublin Review*, xv (1843), 387–415.

Review of *Life of Gerald Griffin Esq.*, *by his Brother*, *Monthly Review*, 162 (1843), 540–3.

Review of *Life of Gerald Griffin Esq.*, *by his Brother*, *Dublin University Magazine*, XXIII (Feb. 1844), 157–70.

Karl von Killinger (trans.), *Gerald Griffin en Schriftstellerleben*, Stuttgart and Tübingen, 1847.

J.W.C., 'The Dramatic Writers of Ireland – No. IX', *Dublin University Magazine*, XLVI (Nov. 1855), 548–65.

N.J.G., 'A Quartette of Irish Poets', *Irish Quarterly Review*, v (Dec. 1855), 697–731.

Daniel Griffin, *The Life of Gerald Griffin*, Dublin, 1857.

J.V.H., Review of *The Complete Works of Gerald Griffin*, *Brownson's Quarterly Review* (July 1859), 342–72.

'National Tintings. I: Gerald Griffin', *Illustrated Dublin Journal*, 5 (Oct. 5, 1861), 65–8.

Review of *The Works of Gerald Griffin in ten Vols.*, *The Christian Examiner*, LXXVIII (May 1865), 346–68.

J. G. McGee, 'Gerald Griffin', *Catholic World*, II (1870), 398–411.

J. G. McGee, Review of *The Works of Gerald Griffin*, *Catholic World*, II (1870), 667–79.

'Prester John', 'Gerald Griffin', *Dublin University Magazine*, LXXXIX (April 1877), 534–41.

'Gerald Griffin', *Cabinet of Irish Literature*, III, London, 1880, pp. 58–60.

P. J. Neilan, 'Notable Irish Writers: Gerald Griffin', *The Nation*, XLIII, 17 (April 25, 1885), 10–11, XLIII, 18 (May 2, 1885), 9–10; XLIII, 19 (May 9, 1885), 10–11.

Lucy C. Lillie, 'The Author of *The Collegians*', *Lippincott's Magazine*, 45 (1890), 395–406.

James Hayes, 'Adventures of an Irish Giant', *The Bookworm*, V, 41 (1892), 6–7.

T. E. Galt-Gamble, 'Footsteps of the Colleen Bawn', *New Ireland Review*, VI (Sept. 1896), 27–38.

'Ignotus', 'Characteristics of Gerald Griffin', *Irish Ecclesiastical Record*, 4th series, IV (Oct. 1898), 297–312.

R. P. Carton, 'The Palace of Art', *Irish Monthly*, XXVII (Oct. 1899), 520–7.

Rose Kavanagh, 'Gerald Griffin's Life and Poetry', *Irish Monthly*, XXVIII (Jan. 1900), 15–27.

Catalogue of Gerald Griffin Memorial Library, Wicklow County Library, Enniskerry, Co. Wicklow, 1901.

Charles Hiatt, 'Gerald Griffin', *Notes and Queries*, 9th series, IX (June 28, 1902), 508.

W. R. Barker, 'Gerald Griffin', *Notes and Queries*, 9th series, X (July 12, 1902), 36.

E. P. Stanton, 'Gerald Griffin', *American Catholic Quarterly Review*, 30 (1903), 283–300.

J.D.B., 'Gerald Griffin as a Christian Brother', *Souvenir of the Centenary of Gerald Griffin*, Cork, 1903, pp. 43–63.

M. McPolin, 'Gerald Griffin', *New Ireland Review*, XXXIII (1910), 89–100.

M. L. R. Breslar, 'Gerald Griffin', *Notes and Queries*, 12th series, I (March 4, 1916), 190.

'St Swithin', 'Gerald Griffin', *Notes and Queries*, 12th series, I (April 8, 1916), 298.

J. J. Kelly, 'Gerald Griffin', *Irish Ecclesiastical Record*, 5th series, VIII (July 1916), 10–34.

Br. D. J. Ryan, 'Gerald Griffin, Poet, Novelist and Christian Brother', *Golden Jubilee Souvenir of Belfast Christian Brothers' Schools*, 1916, pp. 145–7.

Padraic Colum, Introduction to *The Collegians*, Dublin, 1918.

P. Barrett, 'The Colleen Bawn', *Golden Jubilee Souvenir of Christian Brothers*, Kilrush, Co. Clare, 1924, pp. 82–7.

D. Coppinger, *Gerald Griffin*, Dublin, 1930.

D. J. Ryan, *Gerald Griffin: Reasons For His Faith*, Dublin, 1934.

W. S. Gill, *Gerald Griffin, Poet, Novelist, Christian Brother*, Dublin, 1940.

M. Moloney, 'Limerick and Gerald Griffin', *North Munster Antiquarian Journal*, II, 1 (Spring 1940), 4–11.

Maire O'Donovan, 'Gerald Griffin's Nieces', *North Munster Antiquarian Journal*, II, 1 (Spring 1940), 11–13.

R.H., 'Gerald Griffin Centenary', *North Munster Antiquarian Journal*, II, 2 (Autumn 1940), 92.

B. G. MacCarthy, 'Irish Regional Novelists of the Early Nineteenth Century', *The Dublin Magazine*, N.S. XXI, 3 (July–Sept. 1946), 28–37.

Donald Davie, 'Gerald Griffin's "The Collegians"', *The Dublin Magazine*, N.S. XXVIII, 2 (April–June 1953), 23–31.

Ethel Mannin, *Two Studies in Integrity*, London, 1954, pp. 17–132.

Thomas Flanagan, *The Irish Novelists 1800–1850*, New York, 1959, pp. 205–51.

Ethel Mannin, *Loneliness*, London, 1966, pp. 66–89.

John Cronin, 'Gerald Griffin and *The Collegians*: A Reconsideration', *University Review*, V, i (Spring 1968), 57–63.

John Cronin, 'Gerald Griffin's Common-Place Book A', *Eire-Ireland*, IV, iii (Autumn 1969), 22–37.

John Cronin, 'Gerald Griffin: Dedalus Manqué', *Studies*, LVIII, 231 (Autumn 1969), 267–78.

John Cronin, 'Gerald Griffin: A Forgotten Novel', *Eire-Ireland*, V, iii (Autumn 1970), 32–9.

John Cronin, 'The Passionate Perfectionist', *Hibernia*, XXXVI, 5 (March 5–18, 1971), 16.

John Cronin, 'A Select List of Works Concerning Gerald Griffin', *Irish Booklore*, I, 2 (Aug. 1971), 150–6.

John Cronin, 'Gerald Griffin in London, 1823–1827', *Irish Booklore*, II, 1 (Spring 1972), 116–41.

Benedict Kiely, 'The Two Masks of Gerald Griffin', *Studies*, LXI, 243 (Autumn 1972), 241–51.

John Cronin, 'Some Unpublished Letters of Gerald Griffin', *Eire-Ireland*, IX, iv (Winter 1974), 42–68.

John Cronin, 'Macready, Griffin, and the Tragedy *Gisippus*', *Eire-Ireland*, XI, i (Spring 1976), 34–44.

Grace Eckley, 'Griffin's Irish Tragedy, *The Collegians* and Dreiser's *American Tragedy*', *Eire 19*, 1 (Aug. 3, 1977), 39–45.

OTHER SECONDARY SOURCES

Allott, Miriam, *Novelists on the Novel*, London, 1959.

Banim, John, *Damon and Pythias*, London, 1821.
The Boyne Water, 3 vols., London, 1826.
Banim, John and Michael, *Tales by the O'Hara Family*, 3 vols., London, 1825; 3 vols., London, 1826.
Barrington, Sir Jonah, *The Rise and Fall of the Irish Nation*, Paris, 1833.
Beckett, J. C. *The Making of Modern Ireland 1603–1923*, London, 1966.
Brooke, Stopford and Rolleston, T. W. *A Treasury of Irish Poetry in the English Tongue*, London, 1900.
Brown, Stephen, S. J. *Ireland in Fiction: A Guide to Irish Tales, Romance and Folk-Lore*, Dublin, 1916.
Bulwer Lytton, Edward, *Letters of Bulwer Lytton to Macready*, ed. Brander Matthews, Newark, New Jersey, 1911.
Corkery, Daniel, *The Hidden Ireland*, Dublin, 1925.
Synge and Anglo-Irish Literature, Cork, 1931.
Crowley, D. O. (ed.), *Irish Poets and Novelists*, San Francisco, 1893.
Curtis, Edmund, *A History of Ireland*, London, 1936.
DeVere, Sir Aubrey, *English Misrule and Irish Misdeeds*, London, 1848. *Recollections of Aubrey deVere*, London, 1897.
Dickens, Charles, *The Letters of Charles Dickens*, I, ed. Madeline House and Graham Storey, Oxford, 1965.
Doran, John, *Annals of the English Stage from Thomas Betterton to Edmund Kean*, London, 1888.
Dowling, P. J. *The Hedge Schools of Ireland*, rev. edn., Cork, 1968.
Ebers, John, *Seven Years of the King's Theatre*, London, 1828.
Edgcumbe, Fred (ed.), *Letters of Fanny Brawne to Fanny Keats (1820–1824)*, London, 1936.
Edgeworth, Maria, *Life and Letters of Maria Edgeworth*, 2 vols., ed. A. J. C. Hare, London, 1894.
Fitzgerald, Percy H. *The Romance of the English Stage*, 2 vols., London, 1874.
Forster, J. *Life of Oliver Goldsmith*, London, 1903.
Genest, John, *Some Account of the English Stage, from the Restoration in 1660 to 1830*, Bath, 1832.
Griffin, William and Daniel, *Medical and Physiological Problems*, London, 1845.
Gwynn, Denis, *The Struggle for Catholic Emancipation, 1750–1829*, London, 1928.
Houghton, Walter Edwards (ed.), *Wellesley Index to Victorian Periodicals, 1824–1900*, Toronto, 1966.
Joyce, James, *Exiles*, London, 1918.
A Portrait of the Artist as a Young Man, New York, 1916.
Ulysses, Paris 1922.
Kelly, Michael, *Reminiscences of Michael Kelly, of the King's Theatre and Theatre Royal, Drury Lane*, London, 1826.

Bibliography 159

Knowles, James Sheridan, *The Dramatic Works*, 2 vols., London, 1856.
Krans, Horatio Sheafe, *Irish Life in Irish Fiction*, New York, 1903.
Krause, David (ed.), *The Dolmen Boucicault*, Dublin, 1964.
Law, Hugh Alexander, *Anglo-Irish Literature*, Dublin, 1926.
Lover, Samuel, *Poems of Ireland*, London, 1858.
MacCarthy Collins, Charles (ed.), *Celtic Irish Songs and Song-Writers*, London, 1885.
MacDonagh, Thomas, *Literature in Ireland*, Dublin, 1916.
McDowell, R. B. *Irish Public Opinion, 1750–1800*, London, 1944.
Public Opinion and Government Policy in Ireland, 1801–1846, London, 1952.
MacLysaght, W. and Clifford, S. *Death Sails the Shannon*, Tralee, 1953.
Macready, William, *Macready's Reminiscences and Selections from his Diaries and Letters*, ed. Sir Frederick Pollock, London, 1876.
Madden, Richard Robert, *The History of Irish Periodical Literature*, London, 1867.
Maxwell, Constantia, *Dublin Under the Georges (1714–1830)*, London, 1936.
Mitford, Mary Russell, *Recollections of a Literary Life*, 2 vols., London, 1852.
Moore, Thomas, *Memoirs of Captain Rock*, London, 1824.
Memoirs, Journal and Correspondence, ed. Lord John Russell, 8 vols., London, 1853–56.
The Letters of Thomas Moore, ed. W. S. Dowden, 2 vols., Oxford, 1964.
Morgan, Sydney (Lady Morgan), *Memoirs: Autobiography, Diary and Correspondence*, 2 vols., London, 1862.
Murray, Patrick Joseph, *The Life of John Banim*, London, 1857.
Nicoll, Allardyce, *A History of English Drama*, rev. edn., Cambridge, 1946.
O'Brien, George, *The Economic History of Ireland From the Union to the Famine*, London, 1921.
O'Donoghue, D. J. *The Life of William Carleton*, 2 vols., London, 1896.
Sir Walter Scott's Tour in Ireland in 1825, Dublin, 1905.
Oliphant, Margaret, *Literary History of England*, 3 vols., London, 1882.
Poole, W. F. and Fletcher, W. I. *Index to Periodical Literature*, 7 vols., rev. edn, London, 1891.
Power, John, *List of Irish Periodical Publications (Chiefly Literary) from 1729 to the Present Time*, London, A.D. 2000–134 [1866].
Read, Charles A. (ed.), *The Cabinet of Irish Literature*, 4 vols., London, 1879–80.
Roorbach, Orville Augustus, *Bibliotheca Americana*, 4 vols., New York, 1852–61.

Rowell, George, *The Victorian Theatre*, Oxford, 1956.
Scharf, Sir George, *Recollections of the Scenic Effects of the Covent Garden Theatre*, London, 1838.
Scott, Sir Walter, *The Journal of Sir Walter Scott*, ed. W. E. K. Anderson, Oxford, 1972.
Scully, Denys, *A Statement of the Penal Laws*, Dublin, 1812.
Sheil, Richard Lalor, *The Speeches of the Right Honourable Richard Lalor Sheil, M.P.*, ed. T. MacNevin, Dublin, 1845.
Somerville, E. Œ. and Ross, Martin, *The Real Charlotte*, London, 1894.
Strayaways, London, 1920.
Stratman, Carl Joseph, *Bibliography of English Printed Tragedy, 1565–1900*, Carbondale, Illinois, 1966.
Strong, L. A. G. *The Minstrel Boy: A Portrait of Tom Moore*, London, 1937.
Ward, Sir A. W. and Waller, A. R. (eds.), *The Cambridge History of English Literature*, XIII, Cambridge, 1916.
Watson, Ernest Bradlee, *Sheridan to Robertson: A Study of the Nineteenth-Century London Stage*, Cambridge, Mass., 1926.
Watts, A. Alaric, *Scenes of Life and Shades of Character*, London, 1831.
The Laurel and Lyre: Fugitive Poetry of the Nineteenth Century, London, 1867.
A Narrative of His Life, London, 1884.
Wyndham, Henry Saxe, *The Annals of Covent Garden Theatre from 1732–1897*, London, 1906.
Yeats, W. B. *Representative Irish Tales*, 2 vols., New York, 1890.
The Complete Poems, London, 1952.

Index